Because Sometimes a Miracle is a Pussy Willow Tree

by

Lori Sawicki

Tudor Publishers
Greensboro

Because Sometimes a Miracle is a Pussy Willow Tree by
Lori Sawicki © 2002

Printed in the United States

First Edition

Library of Congress Cataloging-in-Publication Data

Sawicki, Lori, 1973—
Because sometimes a miracle is a pussy willow tree/by
Lori Sawicki
p.   c.
Previously published in 1999.
Summary: Fourteen-year-old Darla quickly comes to love
her friend Andy's mother. Mrs. Scully is the wise and kindly
figure she wishes she had for a mother, but it is not until tragedy
strikes that she fully understands the Scully family tradition of
finding miracles in everyday life.
ISBN 0-936389-78-8
[1. Family life—Fiction. 2. Mothers and daughters
Fiction.] I. Title.

PZ.7S2673 Be 2002
[Fic]—dc21   2002190393

This book is dedicated to my husband, Chuck, whose love and friendship help define my life

Special thanks to my Houston editor, sister, and friend, Cheryl Hart, who always believes in me even when I don't. To my niece and favorite young adult reader, Kellie Jo Langley. And to my mom—one of my best friends.

Chapter 1

I didn't really understand about the miracles until after the fire at the Skully's house. Even though the Skullys talked about them a lot, the whole idea of miracles never made a lot of sense to me. Even now, I'm not sure that I understand them the way Mrs. Skully did, but I think I've figured them out for myself, in a way that works for me.

The morning of the orange soda incident, three major things had happened. First, without waking me, my mother left that morning for Europe on a reporting assignment. Second, my father called me at school to say he was stuck in Boston and couldn't come home for another two weeks. Third, I met Andrea Skully.

Two weeks without parents for most kids would be a real kick. But I was feeling pretty lousy that morning, and by lunch really sorry for myself. I never saw my parents enough for it to be much of an adventure when they left, and Mrs. Gorkin, the housekeeper, wasn't much of a conversationalist. Right then, I thought my life was pretty crummy.

So, I was in line at the cafeteria, not paying attention. The cashier asked me twice for the correct change before I realized she was talking to me. After scrambling in my wallet for two extra quarters, I grabbed my tray and moved blindly down the aisle. I do that a lot—walk along without really noticing. It's a bad habit Mrs. Gorkin has been trying to break me of.

Anyway, I thought I heard someone call my name and I turned around thinking it was Stowie, a girl from math class. But when I didn't see her, I swung back around only to collide head on with a girl I'd ever seen before.

If it hadn't been for the orange soda, it might not have been a total disaster, because I only had a wrapped sandwich and a couple of cookies on my tray. But my orange soda seemed to fly out of its cup and all over the shirt of this girl.

Instead of shrieking like I expected her to do, she just looked at me, and then at her shirt and mumbled something about going to the bathroom to clean up. She set her tray down on a table and left quickly—before I had a chance to say anything.

I could have said something, but I was too stunned and surprised and I was feeling lousy enough as it was. Instead, I just went to an empty table and turned my back on the eyes staring at me. I couldn't handle it. It was a bad day.

I'd just started my sandwich when I felt someone standing in front of me. I looked up and saw her. Other than a large orange mark across her blouse, she looked pretty unfazed—not even mad. I knew I should say something but nothing came to mind.

After waiting for a moment, she sat down across from me and introduced herself. "Well, we've sort of unofficially met. I'm Andrea. But everyone calls me Andy."

She had reddish-brown hair and calm eyes. After having orange soda dumped down the front of her blouse, it was sort of amazing that she wasn't more upset. She wore her hair in a bowl cut look, and her blouse was tucked into a pair of jeans. The neatness of her, even after the orange soda incident, made me feel messy, and I ran a hand through my usual mass of unruly curls, suddenly uncomfortable.

I finally responded with my version of an apology. "I wish I'd grabbed a Sprite instead. It wouldn't have left such a stain. I'm Darla. Sorry."

"It's okay. At least it gave me a chance to have lunch with someone. First days are always tough."

She said this in a matter-of-fact way, as if being at a new school was an ordinary event, not tough at all.

"Where did you move from?' I asked, trying to sound polite, but not sure I was really interested.

"Akron, Ohio. We just traded one small midwestern town for another."

I stopped chewing my sandwich to look at her. I guess she did interest me a little. No one I knew talked about small midwestern towns, even though we all lived in one. And no one I knew would be so unselfconscious about a large orange stain on her blouse—especially if they were the new kid.

She looked around the cafeteria and then realized her tray was a few tables away. "Just a sec. I left my lunch over there."

And then she did another amazing thing. She got up in front of a bunch of strangers and walked down the aisle with that giant stain on her blouse and picked up her tray while people stared. It didn't seem to bother her in the least.

As she sat back down, she grinned at me with a look that I can only describe as perceptive. "It's okay if you don't want me to sit here. Spilling orange soda on somebody doesn't make you instant friends."

She said it so easily, and without anger, that I could only look at her in surprise. Shaking my head I said, "Why would you think that?"

"Oh, you look a little uncomfortable. And you haven't really said a whole lot. I can move to another table."

As she started to pick up her tray, I found my voice. "No, it's okay. And I don't say much, most of the time."

She considered this and then began to unwrap her sandwich, taking a bite and then a long swallow from a carton of orange juice.

"Here." She handed me the carton, passing me the straw. "Doesn't look like you've got anything to drink there."

I couldn't help but smile. She was really something. And I surprised myself; I took the juice and slurped down half the carton.

Chapter 2

I had Andy in English and gym classes. By the end of her second week at Lincoln, we were good friends. She was bright and funny—everything I wasn't—and seemed able to cope with my quietness. She took me in stride—something not many people are able to do. For a while, I thought it was the "new kid syndrome"—latching onto the first person who was polite. But soon I knew that Andy really liked me just for me.

One day at the beginning of April, while we were sitting outside by a big oak tree at lunch, Andy invited me to her house without really meaning to. "April is such a beautiful month in Michigan," she said one day in between bites of her sandwich. "You should see the apple blossoms on the trees in our yard."

I knew she didn't say it as an invitation, but I surprised myself again. And I think I surprised her too. "I'd love to."

The words sort of hung between us for a moment, and then Andy did what she always did. She smiled easily and nodded. "Good. How about tomorrow after school?"

"Okay."

"My mom's been anxious to meet you."

I felt suddenly nervous. I've never been any good at introductions, and had never really met anyone's family before.

And so I met the Skullys, the next day after school—well most of them—two days before my dad was due back from Philadelphia from another business trip. I was a little nervous about both events. It was always like that when one of my parents came back from a business trip. It wasn't like having an old familiar face walking in the front door. And even though my folks always made a big fuss over seeing me, it was all pretty artificial—sort of like three people who arrive on a planet and can't speak each other's language, but all have to live together.

So by the time we walked into Andy's house, I was pretty quiet. There was too much to say, too many questions to ask, so I didn't say anything. I'm like that a lot—and Andy took my silence in stride, like everything else about me.

The Skullys had moved into a big white farmhouse set back from Green Road, next to an apple orchard with a jillion large apple trees. Andy was right, their blossoms were incredible. The moment I saw them, I fell in love with her house.

As we walked in, a little boy ran past me, followed quickly by another with a squirt gun. I stepped aside to avoid being knocked over by the second boy as he pushed open the screen door and did a kamikaze jump off the front porch.

Andy turned to me with a "this-is-my-life" look and said, "Haley and Ben. Haley had the squirt gun."

"Brothers?"

Andy nodded. "Twins, no less. C'mon. It gets better." I followed close behind while trying to take in the dining room where the boys had nearly run us over. All I had time to see was its very high ceiling and a long table over a woven rug.

"Mom?" Andy yelled, as we went through a swinging door into the kitchen.

"In here," a muffled voice called back, coming from behind a half-open door that led to what I imagined was the pantry.

When she pushed her head through the pantry door and said, "Just a sec," I knew I'd like her right away. She had a quick, easy smile—like Andy's. And I liked the sound of her voice.

After she'd finished whatever she was doing in there, Mrs. Skully came out into the kitchen, wiping her hands on her jeans. She smiled at me immediately. "So you're Darla. It's nice to finally meet you. It's nice to know that Andy's made such a good friend at Lincoln."

It was comforting to know that Andy regarded me as good a friend as I did her—well, at least her mother did. I felt immediately at ease and sat down at the table, almost as if I were one of the family.

As Mrs. Skully talked to me, she moved around the kitchen putting cookies on a plate and pouring three tall glasses of milk. I was surprised when she sat down with us. Things weren't that easy at my house—not that I'd ever brought anyone home. It's just that my mom never got that involved in a conversation with me—much less sat down with me to talk.

We ate cookies and talked for a long time and I watched how easy Andy and her mom got along. We all sat there yacking like old friends, Mrs. Skully asking me a lot of questions without being phony or intrusive. She talked to me—to the both of us—like we were real people, not just kids.

"You know, Darla, my mother had hair like yours. You'd never know it from mine. I can barely get a curl out of it. And Andy's, well, let's just say she didn't get her hair from my mom's side of the family."

I felt embarrassed, but not so much that I couldn't answer. "I'd give anything to have hair like Andy's. Mine's all over the place," I said, running my hand a little nervously through my always-tangled mop.

"I'll tell ya a secret," Mrs. Skully said, winking at me as she stood up from the table, pulling a carton of milk from the refrigerator. "All us women think there's something wrong with us. If it's not our hair, it's the size of our thighs or hips, or our eyelashes aren't long enough, or we're not pretty enough." She refilled our glasses as she talked and I watched her, sure that I'd never liked anyone I didn't know, so much and so fast.

"It takes years to learn we're pretty darned good the way we are," she said. "You've got to start young. Telling yourself. Believing it. You and Andy are beautiful—inside and out."

My face must have reflected the question that was on my mind—how can you tell I'm beautiful inside?—because she answered it with a warm smile. "I've raised five children and known a lot of their friends. I can usually spot the ones I hope my children stay friends with."

I wasn't sure if it was the way she'd said "us women"—sort of including me in a circle I'd never been in before—or whether it was the way she assured me that I was one of the "friends" she hoped Andy would hang onto, but I can still remember that conversation almost word for word.

It wasn't that she said anything profound. And she wasn't particularly funny or dynamic or anything. But she wasn't critical, either. And her eyes. There wasn't anything particularly unique about them either. But they were kind eyes. And they took me in the way I was—like Andy had, only in an older, more protective way. It was as if I could know her heart from the way she looked at me. And Mrs. Skully never proved me wrong either. For as long as I knew her, and for as long as she was my friend, her kindness to me never changed. I could count on it the way I counted on my parents to leave on business trips every month. Even today, she sends me a Christmas card.

I think I loved Mrs. Skully by the time I left that day. I knew that I could talk to her, and trust her, even though I hadn't talked that much. I remember wishing as I left that night that my mom was more like Mrs. Skully. Or maybe I wished Mrs. Skully was my mother. I guess it didn't matter which. It was obvious that Andy's mom was just about the greatest person I'd ever met.

Chapter 3

I'd been hanging around the Skully's house for a couple of weeks when I first learned about the miracles. It was just before Easter and we were on a short break from school. Both my parents had promised to be home for the long weekend but, as usual, were in business meetings and couldn't get home in time. So Andy invited me to a barbeque at her house.

At first I was really nervous—not that I didn't want to go, mind you. But it was the first time I was going to sleep over at the Skully's. My mom made a big production out of getting the phone number and promising to call to make sure the Skullys were upstanding citizens or something. I don't really think she was as worried about the Skully's reputation as her own—and what they might think of her pawning her kid off on them for the weekend.

I was surprised when she called—from London—a place called Piccadilly Circus. She was on her way to review some play and had stopped off to make the call. I wasn't sure how I felt about that, but she actually talked to me for quite a long time, assured me she'd be home soon, and gave her best to the Skullys.

The barbeque was pretty chaotic, but wonderful. It was an unusually warm weekend and they held the barbeque outside under a big oak tree in the back yard. Mrs. Skully really put on a spread. And everyone helped—so different from the rare family meals we had that Mrs. Gorkin prepared for us at our house. I rarely stepped foot inside our kitchen except for when

I'd sneak down late at night for a snack. On mornings when Mrs. Gorkin found a dirty plate in the sink, she'd shake her head and mutter, "That girl's got insomnia like I've never seen." But of course no one was ever really paying attention. If Dad were home, his face would be hidden behind a newspaper, and Mom would be half at the table, half in the bathroom putting on makeup. So the Skully's family barbeque was a new experience for me.

And I certainly wasn't treated like a guest. Mr. Skully had me peeling potatoes, taking plates out to the picnic table in the back yard and digging in the pantry to find extra mayonnaise.

"Darla, while you're in there, see if you can find another can of cherry pie filling. This cobbler looks a little skimpy."

"Sure, Mrs. Skully," I said, as I went to find the mayo.

"Ben, Haley, I want you both to come over here." The boys stopped, then walked to their mother. "I want you to go outside and see if you can find some flowers for our table."

Immediately they started giggling, and turned to each other holding their noses. "Eeeww! Flowers. They stink up the whole table." But they scurried off, racing each other out the door. I caught a knowing look pass between Mrs. Skully and Andy, who was finishing up the hamburger patties.

It was just a smile. And if I hadn't been watching, I'd have missed it. But it was so full of history, and understanding between them. Maybe it was a mother-daughter moment—I don't know, but I felt momentarily sad and somehow empty. I turned away quickly and busied myself opening the can of cherries when Mrs. Skully, in her usual way, pulled me back into the circle from which she had unknowingly left me out.

"Darla, it's really nice to have you with us this weekend. I don't think Andy's ever had a friend that I've liked so much."

I cut my finger on the cherry can lid as she said it. She and Andy made a big fuss rinsing it and bandaging it. I was glad for the commotion; I wouldn't have known what to say.

It was at the picnc table when the subject of the miracles

came up. And it was all because Jason was in a bad mood. Jason and Lee were Andy's other two brothers. Lee was in the fifth grade and Jason was a little older than Andy and me. They never said much to me, but they seemed nice enough.

After we'd all sat down to eat, the conversation was loud and there seemed to be a lot of activity with food—bowls and plates being passed in every direction. I'm still not sure how the argument started, but suddenly the table got very quiet.

"Haley, can't you ever sit still?" It was Jason, giving his brother more than just a disapproving look. "You spilled milk on me!" Jason stood up and began to wipe up the milk with his napkin. Mrs. Skully started to say something, but he interrupted. "Dad! Can't you control these two? They drive me crazy!" As Mrs. Skully got up to go into the house, she said, "There's no need to bring Ben into this. He didn't do it." She said this calmly. Almost quietly. But I could hear a note of caution in her voice.

But it seemed Jason had had enough. "Last night it was the green beans—Haley threw one at Ben, and then a food fight started. The night before that, Ben served up his whole plate to the dog and spilled half of it on the floor. Can't we have any peace around here? Can't we live like civilized people?" Jason's face had grown bright red; flushed both in anger and, I suspected, embarrassment.

Mrs. Skully came back to the table with a fistful of paper towels. Hearing his last comment, she began to wipe up the milk around his plate, her brows pulled tightly together. "What's bothering you, Jason?" Again, that calm. I took a bite of potato salad and pretended I wasn't there.

"Nothing more than everything else that bothers me around here," he said, sounding a little childish. "Nobody ever makes these two mind. They're out of control." Jason sat back down reluctantly at the table, looking as if he wanted to be anywhere but with all of us.

"Jenny's going out with Bob Greeley," Haley sneered, sticking his tongue out at Jason. "That's why he's such a grouch."

"You creep," Jason snapped, reaching for the twin across the table. I thought he was going to hit him. "That's enough," Mr. Skully said, stopping the argument. Mrs. Skully gave her husband a look that I couldn't read, but something passed between them. "Seems you've been on edge a lot lately, Jason. Maybe," she said, turning Jason's milk glass over and refilling it, "you need to go find a miracle."

I looked up to see the quiet stares of the Skully family on Jason. "Oh, Mom," he protested. "I don't need to—"

"No," she interrupted. "I think you do. Why don't you go now and look for one?

"But I'll miss the rest of the barbeque." He sounded quieter now, his voice losing the whine it had taken on earlier.

"Seems like you've already spoiled it for yourself as it is. There'll be plenty for you when you get back. I'll keep a plate for you."

With that, Jason got up and went into the house, letting the screen door slam behind him. Within a short time he was back, coming down the back steps with a Polaroid camera in his hands. I waited barely breathing, trying to get Andy's attention. My eyes were shouting at her to look at me. But instead everyone went back to eating as Jason walked down the drive-way and out of sight. Soon the conversation started up again. The barbeque ended with Mrs. Skully bringing out the cherry cobbler and slicing up a square for everyone.

I never asked Andy or Mrs. Skully to explain about the miracles, at least not that day. Jason came back to the house about an hour later looking a lot calmer and holding a pussy willow branch in his hand. The white furry tips had long since exploded into yellow caterpillar-like balls, but everyone made a fuss over it anyway. Mrs. Skully took the Polaroid from Jason and took a picture of the pussy willows, and put the picture into what the Skullys called the "miracle book."

Mrs. Skully exclaimed that Jason had found a "beautiful miracle" and that he must've searched long and hard, because

she had never known there to be a pussy willow tree on the
farm, and that it was her favorite spring blossom. Everyone nodded
in agreement. I felt a little embarrassed that I didn't get it. I
mean, it all seemed to be sort of a family thing, but I couldn't
understand how a pussy willow branch, much less a pussy willow
tree, could be interpreted as a miracle. It wasn't until much
later, after the fire, that I came to understand why.

Chapter 4

We found the hidden letter Tuesday morning—the day after the long weekend—that ended up taking us on some pretty interesting adventures, and that eventually led us to the Mason's miracle book. But that comes later. We found the letter because I spent the entire three-day weekend with the Skullys. I called Mrs. Gorkin and told her she didn't have to come by and cook for me. I think she was relieved that I was with Andy, though she'd never met her.

So Tuesday morning, we went to stand at the end of Andy's drive to wait for the bus. When it started to rain it didn't just sprinkle—it started pouring. Neither of us had an umbrella, so we ducked into what Andy called an old rain shack—a bus stop, I guess—that stood off to the side at the end of the driveway. It smelled of old, tired boards and sounded pretty creaky as we came barreling into it.

"Mom told me that she had one of these where she grew up," Andy said. "She used to stand in it on rainy days or really cold, snowy days and wait for her ride to school."

"Looks like nobody's used it for a while," I said, wrinkling up my nose at the musty smell and the paint peeling off the walls. It was big enough for four people to stand in—maybe even wide enough for them not to get claustrophobic—with a strip of what was once white, wide wooden trim around the middle of each wall. It made the walls look cut in half.

"Probably not," Andy answered, standing on her tiptoes to see if she could look out the small window on the side. "Here, give me a boost."

17

I put my bookbag down on the floor and cupped my hands together, bending down so that Andy could step into them. She bounced up a little on her other foot and leaned against the wall. "Seems kind of high for a window," she commented, not noticing that she was starting to wobble and my hands were about to break. "Doesn't seem like you'd be able to see the school bus coming at all."

Just then, my hands gave out and Andy tipped a little too far to the side. We both came tumbling down, Andy on top of me, as we crashed against the opposite wall and hit the floor together.

"Oooww," we both howled, rubbing our heads and arms.

"Are you all right?" Andy asked, crawling off of me, and then starting to laugh.

"What's so funny?" I asked, getting to my feet.

"Us. Definitely coordinated, don't ya think? Should we try out for the basketball team?"

Andy was always saying stuff like that—making the best out of the worst possible thing—and I grinned. As we stood up and brushed each other off, it was then that I saw a part of the en-velope hanging out from beneath the trim on the side of the wall where we'd fallen.

"Look at that," I said to Andy, pointing.

"Wow!" Andy exclaimed, as she pulled the envelope out through the bottom of the wood trim. "It looks like somebody's old letter!"

We moved closer to the entrance of the old rain shack, holding the letter toward the gray, rainy light of the morning. It was addressed to Lexie Montgomery.

"Do you know anyone named Lexie?" I asked Andy, taking the envelope and holding it up in the air.

"My mom's maiden name was Montgomery, but I've never heard of any Lexie."

"The letter's still in there." Andy smiled, giving me a "are-you-thinking-what-I'm-thinking?" look. I smiled back.

We tore open the envelope and read the letter together. It was addressed to Lexie—the girl we didn't know.

April 14, 1959

Dear Lexie,

Only fourteen days till you get here! I can't wait. Mom fixed up the spare bedroom and put a new quilt on your bed. Your room will be right next door to mine. We can stay up late and tell stories, and it's going to be a great spring break.

Buckie had puppies last month and they are so cute. Eight of them! Dad said that was quite a big litter. She had them all over the barn. Every one in a different spot. We even found one behind Dad's lawnmower on the cold, cement floor. You'd think she could've at least had them someplace warm.

My dad's been really cranky lately. Mom says he's impossible. Something's been going on at his work, and I've never seen him like this. He's been miserable to live with. Can you believe it? Mom made him go on a miracle hunt last week. My dad! He's actually got an entry now in the miracle book. I hope he snaps out of it by the time you get here.

Mom's had us doing spring cleaning this week. Everything is being either washed, beaten, polished, or thrown out. Whew! We've gotten into every corner of the house, piece of furniture, and room. Mom's new sideboard never looked so clean. Mom even made us dust the china! Be sure to mention how great the place looks when you arrive. Brownie points with Mom! Maybe she'll let you stay the extra weekend. See you soon.

Love,
Katy-did

We were both quiet for a minute and then we started talking at once. "Who is Katy-did?" I wondered aloud. "What's a Katy-did?"

"Who is Lexie?" Andy said, more to the point. "I bet Mom will know. This house was her Aunt Dorothy's. Did you get that part about the miracle book?"

I was more than surprised—especially because I had witnessed a miracle hunt that weekend at the Skullys and didn't have a clue as to what it was all about. "What is it? Some kind of family tradition?"

"Don't know," Andy answered me distractedly as she re-read the letter. "Wow! I bet my Mom knows who this is. I'll ask her when I get home."

"Promise you'll wait for me! I want to be there too."

We both heard the squeal of the brakes as the bus stopped to pick up the Clefton twins. As a crack of thunder rolled overhead, the bus came into view and stopped at the end of Andy's drive. "Promise!" I yelled as we made a run for the bus.

"Promise," she called back to me. "Come on!"

Chapter 5

When we showed the letter to Mrs. Skully that night, we were in the kitchen getting some snacks. We were all going to watch a movie together on cable and the twins were begging for popcorn. Mrs. Skully had pulled the popper out from the cupboard above the sink and was busy getting the butter and salt when we jumped right in and pushed the letter at her.

I'll never forget the look on her face. Happy and sad at the same time. She read it through silently, then looked up at us with questions. "You said you found this in the old rain shack at the end of the drive? Where?"

Andy and I looked at each other and grinned. "It's a long story, Mom. It must've fallen behind a space in the trim board, and we sort of, well, dislodged it." We both started laughing like crazy.

Mrs. Skully looked at the letter, but her eyes were far away. She stared at it a long time, a remembering smile on her face.

"Mom?" Andy asked, interrupting and taking the letter gently from her mom's hands. "Can you fill us in? Who is Katy-did, and who is Lexie?"

Mrs. Skully smiled a long, slow smile, as if she held a secret, then sat at the kitchen table. As we sat down and Andy grabbed a bag of chips off the counter, placing it between us on the table.

"Mom?" Andy tried again.

"Well, Katy-did is your second cousin and I'm Lexie." She said this nostalgically, that same smile on her lips

"Lexie? Mom, your name is Alexandrea—"

"Uh huh," she answered. "Lexie for short. And Katy, Aunt Dorothy's daughter, was Katrina Amelia Mason."

21

"You never told me that, Mom."

"I guess you don't know everything about me, honey," Mrs Skully answered, smiling.

"Katy-did," I said. "A nickname, too?"

Mrs. Skully grinned at the tone in my voice—a tone that said, "Your family has a lot of nicknames."

"Yes, Darla, yet another nickname." She paused and stared off into space, again coming back to us only as Andy touched her hand. "Mom?"

"Katy and I were very close when I was growing up. Well, you know that," she said, giving Andy a warm smile. "My parents didn't have much money, but Aunt Dorothy—my mom's sister—and Uncle Glenn were a little better off. They lived on this farm, which did very well for many years, and they used to invite me out for visits and vacations. I used to spend weeks at a time out here during the summer. Katy was a few years younger than I was, but we were almost like sisters. You know, Andy, I've told you about some of the summers I spent here."

Andy nodded, munching on a chip, thinking about yet another generation of Skullys living in this house—well, technically, Mason family members. "Do you remember this letter?" I asked. "I mean, I know you never got it, but do you remember this vacation? When you went to visit Katy-did the year Buckie had puppies?"

Another of those smiles. "Oh, yes. I remember it. We had a lot of fun with those puppies. We named all eight of them, really weird names, as I recall."

"Like what?" Andy was amused.

"Hmm, well, we *did* name a few of them sort of normal names. There was Trixie and Duke and Duchess."

"Those sound pretty common," I agreed.

"But there was Wisp, because he was entirely black—black as night—and one named Lion, because he pranced when he walked and crossed his paws when he slept and was all blond. And we named another Can-Can because he never seemed to be able to walk very straight and it looked like he was dancing before he'd fall over. Oh, they were so cute. I do indeed remember that summer."

"Well, it sure sounded like Katy was looking forward to it." I bit into another chip, watching Mrs. Skully like more of a person, maybe, instead of a mom.

"Like I said, we were very close. I was very close to both of them—Katy-did and Aunt Dorothy." She was quiet for a moment, looking around the ktichen. I could tell she was seeing the past as she looked. "It was really hard for me when they both were killed last year. The accident was a real shock."

Andy reached out and touched her arm, and I looked at Andy, a little helpless, not knowing this story and not so sure I wanted to—or should. But Mrs. Skully acted as though she wanted to talk about it, and continued.

"Uncle Glenn died when Katy went off to college, so Aunt Dorothy was often alone. But she and Katy kept in close contact—although Katy was at Purdue University in Indiana. Aunt Dorothy was always excited when Katy came home to visit.

"It was still that way after Katy got a job and moved to Chicago. They talked on the phone all the time. Even after Katy got married, she still came home on holidays."

"Did you stay in contact with Katy?" I asked quietly, wanting Mrs. Skully to know that I was paying attention and cared about her story.

"Oh yes. We wrote all the time, and called. We especially talked a lot after she got divorced. It was a hard time for her then." She stopped talking, taking a chip from the bag, blinking back tears. Andy finished the story for her.

"Last year, in late March, Katy had come home for Easter. It came early that year and there was a snowstorm here. Do you remember it, Darla?"

I nodded. "My dad got stuck in Boston on his flight home from England. And Mom was stuck in California. I was alone for a few days. Even Mrs. Gorkin couldn't get to our house."

Andy continued. "From what the reports said and from what anyone could figure out, Katy and her mom had shopped at the mall most of the afternoon and then tried to drive home in the snow. They had just gotten to the highway and were hit by a semi that slid out of control on the ice."

"Oh my gosh," I said, my mouth unable to chew the rest of the chip I'd bitten into "That's horrible."

"They were both killed," Mrs. Skully finished, got up and filled a glass of water from the faucet. I think she wanted us to believe she was extra thirsty after all those chips, but I really think she didn't want us to see how upset she was.

I tried to keep the conversation moving so that Mrs. Skully could pull herself together. "And you came to live here after they died?"

"Aunt Dorothy left the house to Mom. Well, there was a prov—prov—"

"A provision," Mrs. Skully supplied the word. "A provision in the will. Aunt Dorothy had left the house and the farm to Katy. But in the event that she couldn't take it or didn't want it or something happened to her, she left it to me."

We were silent. The accident felt so big, and the house—as a gift—seemed sort of overwhelming. I could tell that Mrs. Skully felt that way too—like she was grateful for the gift, because she had been so close to them and the farm was like her second home, but that she was really sorry for the way it came to her. That it was hard to accept. Standing there, leaning against the kitchen sink, Mrs. Skully looked a little sick. She seemed momentarily torn up and I got up impulsively and hugged her.

"I'm sorry," I whispered.

"Thank you, Darla," she said as she hugged me back.

"Sometimes it's just still so hard," said Andy. "We agreed to move to the farm. Dad wasn't really happy with his job and Mom had wanted a bigger house. But it took a while to get everything settled. We didn't get here until this spring. The day you spilled your pop on me—remember? Around that time."

I laughed at the memory and Andy did too. And Mrs. Skully smiled as well, despite how sad she must have been feeling. "I remember you coming home with that orange stain on your blouse, Andy," she said, the mood lightening a little as she sat back down. "Who'd have thought that the person you bumped into that day would become your best friend?"

They looked at me and I felt more a part of the Skully family than before. Suddenly I felt like I knew Aunt Dorothy and Katy, some of the childhood they had shared: the puppies, and how they must have stayed up talking and giggling during their vacation. I could feel their laughter and their conversation in the kitchen as we sat there, and partly came to understand why Mrs. Skully always seemed so comfortable here—as if she belonged in the pantry, digging around for a bag of flour or another can of peaches. In so many ways, it had been her home, and she'd shared it with people she loved dearly and lost. Maybe it was a mixture of those feelings that made me want to find Aunt Dorothy's miracle book. Suddenly, as if touching Mrs. Skully's past would keep me firmly implanted in the Skully's present.

Chapter 6

Before we had a chance to look for the Mason's miracle book, I turned fourteen. My parents were in California on my birthday, so I woke that morning to find a new ten-speed bike in the living room with a huge white bow around it and a card woven into the back spokes. In it was a check for a hundred dollars. Although I knew my parents would call me, I decided I didn't want to hang around the house waiting for them. So I hopped on my new bike and rode over to Andy's.

We were hanging out on the front porch, enjoying the fact that school was out, and talking about what I should buy with my birthday money when Andy got a phone call. Just as she went inside, Mrs. Skully came out and joined me on the porch swing. She had a scrapbook with her—one I'd seen her working on before—and a tin full of old pictures.

As she sat down, Mrs. Skully handed me a card that said, "Happy Birthday, Darla" on the envelope, and then began looking in the tin for just the right picture for the page she was on.

I didn't know what to say, so I opened the card. It said: "To a very special person," on the front. On the inside the poem read:

"You're not exactly family,
But you've been more than just our guest.
You've shared a lot of family things,
And been there for all the rest.
So on this special birthday,
This wish is just for you.

We wish you all of life's best things,
For all the whole year through."
Love, Mrs. Skully

Before I knew what was happening, I was crying all over the place, wiping my nose on my shirt sleeve. Mrs. Skully stopped working on her pictures and gave me a hug.

"What is it, Darla?"

In just those few words, she seemed to touch every vulnerable spot inside me. And I wanted to flood out my feelings about how I hated my life, and my house, and how I wished I had a family like Andy's. And how I felt miserable most of the time unless I was with Andy at her house, and how I loved their front porch swing, and that I wished my parents had given me a card like she had instead of a hundred dollar check. And I think all of that tried to come out in the response I gave her. "I just wish," I said, sniffling, "that my mom was more like you." I looked up at her, as I was cradled beneath her arm, and her face had a very quiet, thoughtful look. She sort of gazed out over the yard and at the sky as if she were trying to find just the right words to say to me. I thought maybe she'd say, "I know, Darla. It's hard for you." Or even suggest I come live with them. But instead, she said something I've never forgotten.

"I have a philosophy about people." She spoke in that calm voice that matched her eyes. When I didn't say anything, she continued. "I believe that most often, people try their very best. And even though it may not seem like it at times, it's important to accept their efforts as their best. Even if they don't quite meet your expectations." Then she gave my shoulder a squeeze and went back to her scrapbook. But for once, I was more curious than I was shy.

"What do you mean, Mrs. Skully?"

She hesitated, then said, "Maybe your mom's doing the best she can. Sometimes it's hard to believe it, but maybe she's doing all she knows how to do."

Before I could answer, Andy came bounding out of the door just then, excited and bursting with news. "You'll never guess what! Guess who just called me?!"

I shook my head and made room for her on the swing. But she chose to pace around the porch instead. "Darrel Adams! You know, that guy from math who sits up front. He wants to go to the movies with me!"

Chapter 7

The following Saturday was cold and rainy—a perfect day for snooping around Andy's attic for the Mason's miracle book and for getting the latest scoop on Andy's "date" with Darrel. But we never got around to talking about him, as the search in the attic ended up taking all our attention.

Despite a heavy rain, I rode my bike over to Andy's house, the hood of my jacket pulled tight around my head. I dragged my bike up the stairs, up under the eaves of the wide front porch, parking it next to the door. I knocked once and went in, taking my coat and boots off in the entranceway.

"Gross day, huh?" Andy said, bounding down from upstairs and taking my coat. "Here, just hang it on the hook. Looks like it needs to dry out."

Andy was dressed in jeans and an old T-shirt, and the sides of her hair were pulled back by barrettes. It amazed me how she could always look good—even to scrounge around in a dirty attic. "Come on. Dad helped me with the ladder."

The opening to the attic was through the ceiling in Ben and Haley's room. It was a square hole, about the size of a long dining room table, and was covered by a door with a small latch. Andy's dad had placed a step-ladder under the hole. It looked just about tall enough for us to stand on the top step and pull ourselves through. After seeing it, I was a little surprised that Mr. Skully had agreed to let us explore the attic. Getting there seemed a little dangerous.

"How'd you get your dad to agree to this?" I asked, nodding at the ladder.

"I told him we'd do a little cleaning up there if he'd let us. He'd like to move some of the boxes we never unpacked up there."

"Sounds fair enough," I said, climbing the ladder and pulling on the door latch. The door slid back easily and the smell of musty old things came pouring out.

"Whew! Smells like we'll have a lot to clean."

"Pretty bad?"

"I guess we'll see." I was just tall enough to see up over the side of the opening. I put my arms into the hole and, holding onto the right lip of the opening, I pulled my elbows in close to my sides and pulled myself up and onto the attic floor. I sort of teeter-tottered, my legs hanging down, my body bent at an odd angle, but I was able to pull myself in. I felt like I had just rolled into a giant ball of dust, and stood brushing myself off, sneeziing like crazy.

"Be glad you wore your old clothes," I yelled to Andy.

"Help me up." Andy stood on the top step and held out her hand. I half-pulled, half-yanked her up, Andy using her other hand as a support around the opening of the attic. She landed with a thud on the floor, then stood up, brushing at herself the way I had. It was practically hopeless and we looked at each other, laughing.

"Forget it," I said. "By the looks of it, it'll get worse."

We stood there and took stock. The room ran the length of the house—it was long and narrow. A giant round window on the far wall let in a lot of light and we could see that the place was pretty dirty. But it was sort of exciting. There were a lot of old chests, crates, boxes, a dresser, and what I later learned was an *armoire*, all stacked or positioned against a wall. A floor lamp, a chair, and an old stereo were placed in the middle of the room—as if someone used to come to the attic to read or listen to music. There were shelves of books against one wall and some old records next to them. Under the round window was a bunch of old paintings standing one against the other.

The first one, facing into the room, was of a little girl and her mother dancing in the rain. I walked over to it, carefully picking my way through toys, tools, and boxes scattered on the floor. I took the picture and held it up to Andy.

"Cool, huh? I kind of like this."

"I'm sure Mom wouldn't mind if you kept it," Andy nodded her approval and moved over toward the books.

"I didn't mean that," I said self-consciously. "I didn't come here to get anything; I just thought the picture was neat." I looked at the other pictures, but set the one of the mother and daughter aside. We had a lot of exploring to do to find the miracle book and I realized I was already letting myself get sidetracked.

"Okay," I said, standing with my hands on my hips, "where do we start?"

"I guess anywhere. Why not try that trunk in the corner? We should probably look inside everything with a drawer or a door."

So I walked over to the trunk and knelt down in front of it, forgetting about the dirty floor, and carefully opened the lid. I guess I thought it might be locked or something—like in the movies, where the person has to smash open the lock—but it wasn't like that. It opened like any other lid, except that the hinges squeaked a little bit. Andy started with some boxes near the bookcase.

I gasped when I looked in the chest, feeling for a moment like I *was* in a movie. "What's the matter?" Andy asked from the other side of the room. "Did you find it?"

"No, but look at this."

I carefully pulled out a long ivory wedding dress, holding it up near the shoulders. The silky fabric made a soft rustling sound as it moved against itself and slid easily over the side of the chest. I had to drape the dress over my arm to pull out the train—a simple piece of ivory attached to the back. Once I got it out, I held the dress up again.

"Wow!" Andy said, hurrying over. "This is beautiful. It's

nothing like the dresses you see now. All those beads and sequins and glitter."

"And it's so much prettier."

"I wonder if that was Aunt Dorothy's dress? The one she married Uncle Glenn in."

"Probably. It's beautiful."

"What else is in there?" Andy picked up the train, brushing away a few pieces of dust, and knelt down in front of the chest.

I folded the dress carefully and put it in my lap as I sat down cross-legged next to Andy, who pulled out a box of old pictures and a scrapbook. The scrapbook got us excited, but it ended up being a wedding album—not the miracle book. We looked through it anyway and put it aside, deciding that we'd show it to Andy's mom later.

There were a lot of boxes with old books, and Andy looked through many of them but finally gave up. After digging through them and stacking them on the floor next to the boxes, she eventually sat back on her hands, legs sprawled out in front of her, and sighed.

"It's stupid to look in these," she pointed grumpily at the books. "Nobody'd put a miracle book in with a bunch of old novels."

I nodded. "Maybe it's with some old scrapbooks or photo albums. Anything like that in there?"

Andy shook her head.

"Well, don't get discouraged. It's gotta be up here somewhere. We're just getting started."

"Yeah," Andy answered, gaining back her usual enthusiasm, pushing herself off the floor and brushing at her jeans. "I'll look over here."

She went to the far right of the attic as I continued to look through a small cedar chest that seemed to have been used as a footstool near the chair. There were blankets and some sheets stacked neatly on two pillows and an old quilt on top.

"Did your mom's Aunt Dorothy quilt?" I asked distractedly,

pulling out the quilt and letting it unfold to the floor. It was blue and white, and the patterns made a large diagonal diamond across the front. You could tell it had been done by hand and I commented on how pretty it was.

"Seems like everybody in my family quilts."

"Your mom too?"

"She'd rather sew, actually. But I think she did a quilt once when I was little."

I sat back down, letting the quilt bunch up in my lap. It smelled dusty and tired, but in a good way. I held it against my face, feeling the soft cotton cloth against my cheek. It occurred to me that my mom probably didn't have the vaguest idea what a quilt was—much less how to make one.

The thought made me sad and I sat there staring off into space, feeling that the quilt somehow meant something. Something important. I wondered what it was like to have a family that made quilts—that put one away to keep like this one. I suddenly wanted my mother to see the quilt—touch it, hold it, feel how soft it was—as if someone had used it over and over, and it had been washed over and over until it was so soft and so familiar that you couldn't sleep without it. Part of the comfort of it was that someone had made it for you—with their own hands, piece by piece. A gift of time.

Time. Everything about the attic seemed to be about time. And it wasn't just the smell. There had been family in the things we found in the attic that day. Family and togetherness and memories. These people had memories. They'd made them. I remember looking over at Andy just then, her head stuck behind more boxes, the back half of her sticking out—and I knew that most of my memories would be of her and the Skullys. And of Mrs. Skully, especially, whom I knew I'd never forget as long as I lived. They were my quilt. I felt tears sting my eyes, and I felt really sad.

I don't know how long I sat there, but I snapped out of my thoughts when Andy sat next to me on the dusty floor. She

looked at me and smiled with that knowing smile that was Andy's;
it meant she understood, but without saying it.

"You're pretty far away. Do you want to talk about it?"
I shook my head. "Not really, I guess. It's just the usual
stuff—your family starts to rub off on me."

I didn't have to say anything else and Andy didn't ask.
Sometimes I think we had ESP or something, because I knew
she could read my thoughts and I hers. She gave me a quick
hug as she stood up and went back to the boxes in the corner,
leaving me to get past my feelings and keep looking.

We worked for about forty-five more minutes without luck,
when Andy cried out from the corner, her voice muffled like
she'd swallowed a mouthful of cobwebs.

"Come here, Darla!" she said excitedly as she pulled away
some boxes from around what looked like a small nightstand—
a table whose drawer had a small metal handle on the front and
a keyhole in the middle. There was a shelf on the bottom. An
old lamp sat on the top of it—a long cobweb linking them.

"The drawer's locked, Darla. I can't open it."

"You think it could be in there?" I was catching her excitement. The drawer seemed just the right size.

"Well, look at it. It's the right size, isn't it? And why would
it be locked? Why would anyone put a locked nightstand in
the attic?" She talked fast as she bent to pull at the drawer.

"It won't budge."

"Okay, then where would your mom's Aunt Dorothy hide
the key? If there even still is a key."

"There must be one. Don't people in the movies hide them
under the drawer or tape them to the back of something?" She
bent down, peering under the top of the nightstand, then pulled
it away from the wall, checking the back.

"Nothing," she said, pushing it a little too hard back against
the wall. The lamp on top started to topple and I caught it just
before it went over.

"Oops," I said, grabbing the lamp by the base and reaching

for the shade. I barely managed to keep both from crashing to the floor. I was just about ready to put the lamp back on the nightstand when Andy stopped me.

"Wait a minute! Look."

She pointed to the bottom of the lamp. Holding onto the shade, I sort of tipped it on its side and held it.

"What?"

"The key! Look. The key!"

I put the lamp down on its side on the floor and checked the bottom of the base. Sure enough, it was hollow and taped to one side was a key.

"What a cool hiding place," I said, pulling the key from the underside of the lamp base and peeling off the tape. It felt extra sticky and stuck to my fingers as I handed it to Andy.

"No, you go ahead."

"You saw it first. See if it'll open it."-

Andy took the key a little nervously and bent down to try the key in the lock. It slid in pretty easily and turned right away. Andy looked at me and pulled on the drawer. It opened!

My heart was pounding and I had to laugh a little. It wasn't like we were searching for buried treasure or anything, but for a moment it seemed as if we'd found it. And though I didn't know exactly how Andy felt about it, it seemed very important to me that we find the book. That I get to see someone else's version of a miracle—as if it were still hard to believe that there could be more than one miracle book in the whole world. It seemed like such a big thing in the Skully family—something important. It had become like a mystery or a secret to me—one that I wanted to understand.

As Andy opened the drawer, her face fell. I could tell right away without looking that the book wasn't there. She looked so disappointed that I reached over and touched her arm. "It's okay," I said. "It's only the first day. It's gotta be somewhere in your house."

Andy reached into the drawer and pulled out an address

book, flipping through it without really reading it, and I pulled out a narrow ledger book that had a lot of numbers written in it. I wanted to make sure that Mrs. Skully's Aunt Dorothy hadn't made her miracle book out of it. Other than a pen, some tape, a candle, and a book of matches, the drawer was empty.

"Big reason to lock the drawer," Andy said sarcastically—a tone I didn't hear from her often.

"Well, maybe this was a bank account or something," I answered, tapping the cover of the ledger.

"Yeah, and the address book is filled with names of spies and secret agents."

She tossed the book back into the drawer and turned away with a heavy sigh. "I give up," Andy said with her hands on her hips. "We've been up here forever. I don't think it's here."

I could tell by the way the light was coming in the big round window that it was past lunch. Andy was right; it was probably time to call it quits. Besides, I was getting hungry.

"We didn't clean much," I said. "Will your dad be mad?"

"Nah. We can take a couple of boxes down—maybe the books. He loves to read. I don't think he figured we'd clean the attic for real."

Andy put some of the books she'd looked at in a box and pushed it toward the hole in the floor. "He'll love these."

I stood in the middle of the room, taking a last glance around and found myself looking at the quilt. I hadn't closed the cedar chest and it was hanging out over the side. Andy must have seen me looking at it because she walked over and took it out of the chest, folding it, and holding it over one arm. Before I could say anything, she said in her usual Andy way, "We've been needing another quilt—you know, for when you sleep over. Let's take this one down and wash it up."

I don't think Andy thought I was dumb—as if it escaped me that it was summer and that a quilt like that would be much too hot, or that I didn't realize that the Skullys had plenty of quilts and blankets. I just smiled at her, nodding in agreement.

Chapter 8

The miracles came up again two months into the summer when Darrell "broke up" with Andy. To this day, I can still remember the argument that Andy and Mrs. Skully got into over Andy's behavior and how the search for the miracle seemed to resolve it between them.

"Andy, you've been moping around the house for almost a week. Are you going to tell me what's going on?"

I was sitting on the porch swing reading, trying not to eavesdrop through the open window.

"I told you, nothing. Can't you just leave me alone?"

Mrs. Skully was silent for a few moments considering this comment, then said, "You know, I don't believe you mean that. But for now, if that's what you want, fine. I'm here if you need to talk." It sounded like a nice way for a mom to answer who was probably pretty irritated, but Andy wouldn't let it go.

"Why do you think I don't mean it? Must you know everything? Can't I have any privacy? It's none of your business!"

It was so unlike Andy that I sat gaping at the window. Andy had been pretty touchy around me lately, but friends put up with that sort of thing. But to say those things to your mother, well, it was sort of scary to listen to.

"Andy," Mrs. Skully said in a quiet, controlled voice, "I think you owe me an apology for that." But Andy wouldn't have anything to do with it.

"For what? For being honest? For asking to be left alone?"

"No," Mrs. Skully answered, her voice a little edgy. "For being so rude about it. There are ways to get your point across without being inconsiderate."

"What way, Mom? Like you? So calm, so easy-going about everything? Never get mad? Sorry, but I'm me, not you. And if I feel like getting mad, I should have that right."

I found myself near tears—wanting to run in there and stop them, hug them both; make them hug each other. But I was paralyzed by the silence that followed. I'd never heard Andy sound so nasty. And I knew she must be hurting pretty bad to ever speak to her mom that way. I guess broken love does that to you—but I wouldn't know.

In the silence, I heard one of them move around, and the sound of a door closing. "Andy," Mrs. Skully said without giving away any anger she might be feeling, "I think you need to go search for a miracle."

I heard Andy sigh. "And what if I don't want to go search for one?"

Mrs. Skully's voice sounded stony then. "I'm not sure you want to go down that path with me."

About ten seconds later, Andy came storming through the front door. "C'mon," she said, as she headed down the steps.

"Where're we going?" I pretended I didn't know.

"To find a miracle," she answered sarcastically. "Haven't you been listening?"

I kept up with her as best I could but she was walking at a gallop, and I was red-faced and out of breath when she finally stopped along the path near the park and plopped down in the grass. I didn't know what to say, so I didn't say anything. I just picked at a piece of clover and waited.

"I can't believe he took Sarah Atkinson to the movies!" she exploded, leaning back on her hands, looking up at the sky.

"I wondered when you'd tell me what happened."

She looked at me and smirked. "You sound like my mother."

It must have been the surprised and hurt expression on my face in response to her comment that brought the tears to her eyes. Because she broke down after that and cried a lot, half-apologizing, half-telling me about Darrell in broken sentences, feeling bad about what she had said to her mother. Everything she said was a jumble, and I just sat and listened, nodding my head as if I understood, feeling bad too.

After a while, Andy calmed down. I could tell she must have been bottling this up all week, because it felt like an explosion. She sighed. "My mom's gonna be real mad at me."

"Oh, I don't know," I said quietly. "Your mom'll understand." I wasn't sure about this. I'd never seen Andy and Mrs. Skully argue before, but I thought she'd be okay about it.

"Well, I guess I better find the miracle and get back." She started to get up, but I stopped her.

"Andy, what is it all about? Searching for miracles, I mean. I don't get it."

She sat back down and shrugged. "I think it's Mom's way of getting us to blow off steam. We usually leave the house, and when we come back, we're calmer."

"But what does the miracle part mean?"

She shrugged again. "I don't know exactly. But it kind of diverts our attention looking for one when we're mad, I guess."

I nodded as if I understood, but I was skeptical. Somehow, it seemed that there had to be more to it than that. I mean, Mrs. Skully had them take pictures of each miracle. Pictures of a pussy willow branch, for crying out loud. How was that a miracle? I couldn't guess. I mean, yeah, okay, God may have created it, and God had something to do with miracles, so in a weird way, I guess a pussy willow branch *could* be a miracle. But if that was Mrs. Skully's definition of a miracle, then practically the whole world was a miracle. And that seemed weird.

Andy's search for a miracle ended in her taking a picture of a kite that a couple of kids were flying.

"A kite?" I asked. "How is a kite a miracle?"

"Well, Mom never questions about what we bring back or take pictures of, as long as it's something different or special or unique and that we think about it. Haven't you ever wondered how a kite stays up in the air? I could watch one all day."

She had a point, but I still couldn't see how it could be considered a miracle—I mean, what did God have to do with two kids flying a kite? I started to consider the wonder of wind, but Andy was ready to go back to the house.

When we got back, Mrs. Skully was working on her scrapbook in the kitchen. She smiled as if nothing had happened. "What did you find, Andy?"

Andy showed her mom the picture of the kite and then impulsively hugged her at the same time. "This is nice, Andy. It's a very colorful kite. Did they have it flying really high?"

"Pretty high. Look how long the tail is."

I marveled at how easy they became mother and daughter again, their angry confrontation now apparently forgotten. But the whole day—the whole search for a miracle—stayed with me for a long time. And, as I said before, it really wasn't until the fire that I started to understand what it all meant.

Chapter 9

I don't know why I felt it was so important to find Mrs. Skully's aunt's miracle book. Although Andy seemed excited about it, I think I was more determined. Maybe I thought that by seeing Aunt Dorothy's book, Mrs. Skully's book would become clear—that the whole miracle thing would somehow make sense. Whatever the reason, Andy and I felt the excitement of a "treasure hunt" searching the basement the next Saturday.

"Search for the miracle book—take two," Andy joked. She headed toward some boxes against the wall and I followed.

"Sure you don't remember seeing it when you moved in here?" I asked Andy, pulling at a few boxes. "I mean, if everything was pretty much left the way it was when your mom's aunt died, wouldn't you have run across it by now?"

Andy moved to a cupboard farther down the wall, her answer muffled. "I guess you don't look for something if you don't know about it," she said, coming back into my side of the room. "Nothing in there but some old tools."

"Yeah, but didn't your mom and dad look around—I mean, sort of take inventory of things when you moved in?"

"I guess so. But I doubt a miracle book was on their minds."

Even with the bulbs turned on overhead, the light in the basement was dim, making it difficult to see into corners and search shelves and cupboards. "Gotta flashlight, Andy?"

"Upstairs in the drawer by the phone."

I ran up, found the flashlight and came back down, feeling a little foolish as I peered into boxes and cabinets with the light. I felt like some kind of detective.

41

As if reading my mind, Andy laughed. "Hey, you, the sleuth. Hand that to me for a sec, will ya?"

I gave her a sarcastic smile and the flashlight. "Did you find something?"

"No, I guess not," she said, handing it back to me. "Thought I saw a book there at the back of the shelf, but it's just an old western novel."

We kept searching the basement, stopping to look at pieces of somebody's memories, digging through boxes, but we didn't find the miracle book. There were lots of places to look, but we came up empty. I thought I'd found it after crawling in under the stairwell, finding an old cedar chest against the far wall. It was filled with a lot of old clothes, but the miracle book wasn't in there. It was sort of disappointing, and I crawled out, covered with cobwebs, feeling tired, and the excitement of the adventure was beginning to wear off. I asked Andy if she wanted to call it quits for the day and go for a bike ride.

"Maybe," she answered distractedly, "but come here and look at this first."

"Did you find it?"

"No, not the book. It's an old diary. Look at it; it's even got the little key to the lock taped on the back."

"It looks old," I said, taking it from her and turning it over in my hands. "Should we snoop? I mean, what if it was your mom's aunt's or Katy's? I don't think I'd want someone reading my old diary." But I didn't sound convincing and Andy grinned. We sat down on the basement floor and opened it.

That afternoon turned into an adventure with us spending about an hour reading through the diary. It was Aunt Dorothy's diary, and for a while, it was interesting to see what had been happening back then—when she'd been alive. But soon, news about the weather and financial issues and the crops got to be sort of boring. I began to lose interest when something in one of the entries Andy was reading caught my attention.

April 10, 1957

The weather has been wet and cold. Spring surely is coming in like a lion. Katy has had the flu and I've been up nights
with her.
The most exciting news this week was getting the sideboard
for the dining room. Glenn picked it up cheap at the auction
in town and brought it home in the truck today. It's beautiful.
A nice light oak, finished and shiny. It has two cupboards below,
where I can put my china and a long drawer at the bottom.
I've never seen one I liked so well. Glenn knows my taste and
brought it home as a surprise. He covered my eyes and walked
me out the front door. He said, "Surprise" and pulled my hands
away. There it was. He'd put it on the grass in the front yard.
I cried and gave him a hug. What a devil my Glenn is.

Dorothy

"Isn't that romantic?" Andy asked, sighing a little as she
finished reading the entry.
"What's so romantic about it?" I asked, not really listening,
concentrating on what was bothering me about the entry.
"Well, it's not that he got her a big diamond ring or anything," Andy said almost apologetically, "but you can tell how
much it meant to her that—"
"Andy," I interrupted, "didn't the letter we found in the rain
shack say something about a sideboard?"
"I don't know. I don't remember." She started to turn the
page in the diary, but I stopped her.
"Wait a miute. This is like the second time we've read about
there being a sideboard in this house."
"Okay. I guess I remember something in the letter about
cleaning."
"Yeah! Katy talked about her mom—Aunt Dorothy—doing
spring cleaning and the sideboard looking like new."

"I don't get you."

"Where is that sideboard? I don't remember seeing it in your house anywhere."

Andy started to make the connection. "You're right. And," she paused, nodding her head, "if we find the sideboard—"

"We find the miracle book!" I finished for her. "I mean, doesn't it seem weird that we can't find the book, and we don't know where the sideboard is either?"

"Good point," Andy whispered, as though we'd become the Nancy Drews of the twenty-first century.

"Let's go ask your mom!"

We put the diary back in the cupboard where Andy had found it and ran up the stairs as if we'd seen ghosts in the basement. We ran through the house calling for Mrs. Skully, and were out of breath when we found her in the back yard, weeding one of her flower gardens.

"What's the matter?" Mrs. Skully asked, slightly alarmed.

"We've just got a question to ask you," I jumped in, then looked at Andy.

"Mom," she asked, slowing down to catch her breath, "when we moved here, did Dad move any of Aunt Dorothy's furniture? Where is all her stuff?"

"Well," she answered, pulling off her gloves and wiping her wrist across her forehead, "there really wasn't that much. We moved her double bed into the study for the twins, and we put the dresser in there too."

"But what about the dining room, Mom?" Andy was moving back and forth—nearly hopping from one foot to the next. It was the only sign of impatience I'd ever seen from her.

"We put the dining room table on the screen porch so we could have summer meals out there without mosquitoes. And we took her china and stored it in our hutch, and—"

"That's what I mean! Where did Aunt Dorothy have her china?"

"In the sideboard. We didn't go through it except to move

the dishes. Why the interest in Aunt Dorothy's furniture?" Mrs. Skully looked amused and confused all at the same time.

"That's it!" Andy shouted loudly. She was very excited and I could hardly stand it. "Where is the sideboard?"

"Dad and Mr. Keller next door moved it to the barn. I think he said they covered it with an old tarp."

Andy and I screamed at the same time.

"Thanks, Mom!"

"Thanks, Mrs. Skully!"

I followed Andy, both of us starting to run as we hit the driveway and worked our way around the house and through the back yard. We heard Mrs. Skully yelling to us as we rounded the corner of the house, but neither of us turned. Andy just threw her hand in the air in a quick wave and we kept going.

We ran through the thick grass toward the barn that stood what seemed to be a mile from the house. It was tall and white and looked freshly painted, though I couldn't recall anyone from the Skully family taking on the project recently. As we neared the two doors at the front, we both slowed to a stop, gasping for breath, both trying to talk at once.

"I—I—bet ya anything it's here!" I pointed, pulling on the bolt to open the doors.

"Yeah!—we should—of—looked here sooner." Andy leaned against the door and pushed her bangs away from her forehead. Sweat was running down her face and, thinking that I probably looked the same, I took a swipe at my face with the back of my shirt sleeve.

"Come on, help me with this," I said when my heart had finally stopped pounding. "Help me lift the latch."

A long white piece of wood, bolted on the left door, was lodged between a notch in the door on the right. It lay exactly straight across, holding both doors together. There wasn't a lock, so we lifted the wooden arm up enough to clear the outside of the notch and then pulled forward and let the arm swing down. We pulled on the door at the right. It swung open easily.

The light from the side windows was barely enough to go hunting around the barn. It was huge and filled with old equipment and I was overwhelmed by the size of it. There were stairs leading to a loft overhead, but it didn't make sense that Mr. Skully and Mr. Keller would take the sideboard up there. As my eyes became accustomed to the dim light, I was able to see better what was in the barn. A giant tractor stood smack in the center, its huge wheels taller than Andy and me if I stood on her shoulders. Off to the side were wooden box-like stalls. Once they must have been used to store hay or keep horses, but now they were filled with rakes, shovels, hoses, old tires, and a bunch of other tools and equipment.

The walls were lined with shelves of old paint cans, oil cans, brushes, glass jars of nails and bolts—most of them rusty-looking and old. There was an old workbench along the left wall that ran nearly the length of the barn. It was piled with old wood, tools, and what looked like old car parts. It didn't look like anyone had touched the stuff in years.

Cobwebs lined the corners of two windows—one on the left wall and one on the right. They had pieces of wood strips criss-crossed on them to make it look like there were eight pieces of glass—or maybe there were eight pieces, each set into the wood. It was hard to tell—the windows were a lot higher than Andy and me.

Even though Andy and I had on tennis shoes, our feet made scraping noises on the cement floor. It felt chilly and damp in the barn and though my eyes searched quickly, trying to sort though all the junk, I didn't see anything with a tarp over it—nothing the shape of a sideboard.

"Do you see it?" I sort of whispered.

Andy shook her head. "It's too big not to see it right off. But I don't know where it could be."

We moved to the back of the barn, passing the tractor on the left. At the back was more of the same—it just seemed like a lot of junk. I was starting to feel very disappointed, and I could sense that Andy was, too, when we passed one of the last stalls against the right wall. I was paying more attention to a piece of cloth stretched over a wagon at the back when Andy screamed.

"Darla! There it is!"

Her words echoed loudly against the barn's tall ceiling, and I held myself in waiting for animals to scurry from their nests or birds to start flying around trying to get out. But there was silence after the echoes. Then she whispered. "Look!"

Pointing to the last stall, I could see the tarp through the slats. We hurried over to it and saw that a tarp had been placed over something long and low. Andy pulled at the end of the tarp, which was much heavier than either of us thought a tarp would be. So I took the end, too, and together we pulled hard until it slipped down over the end of the sideboard and to the ground. I looked at Andy and she grinned that grin and we both jumped up and down and hugged each other.

"Come on! Let's look in the cupboards." I still remember the feeling as we opened the doors to the sideboard. When we didn't find the miracle book in there, we opened the long, narrow drawer beneath the doors. And there it was. As Andy pulled it out, we both were quiet, almost afraid to open it. I think Andy was feeling what I was at that moment. This was somebody's special book and maybe it was private—kind of like the diary. But it didn't take long for us to get past that feeling and pull a couple of wooden crates together into the stall. Andy and I sat down and opened Aunt Dorothy's miracle book.

Chapter 10

We sat looking through the miracle book until there was almost no light left in the barn to see by. Sitting side by side on the two old crates, we turned page after page in fascination— as if we were unraveling a mystery. And I guess we were. The first page had bold printing:

The Mason Family Miracle Book
1955
Glenn
Dorothy
Katy

We did the math. It seemed that the Masons started their miracle book when Katy was about eight. I asked Andy when they'd started the Skully miracle book, but she said she didn't really know. That it had just been around for as long as she could remember.

Each page in the Mason's miracle book was covered with a plastic type of slip-on to protect it. They crinkled a little as we turned them; the sound loud in the quiet of the barn.

We looked at each miracle without really saying anything, taking a long time on each page, reading what Mrs. Skully's Aunt Dorothy had written under each one. Once in a while, a particular miracle would make one one of us say, "Look at that one," or "Hmm." Mostly I wanted to say, "I don't get it." But I kept quiet.

Along with other things, the Mason's miracle book held a

four-leaf clover, pressed flat, each small leaf distinctly separate from the others. It had actually stayed sort of green, though the caption said it had been picked in 1957. It was in a very small piece of plastic stapled to the page. There was a picture of a bird's nest with three baby birds in it. The photographer had gotten close and I stopped on that one, feeling for a moment as if I understood it—baby birds, birth, creation—that seemed more like a miracle.

"That looks like it was taken in the bush next to the front porch." Andy peered at it a little more closely. "The wrens made a nest there this year."

There was what looked like an old piece of lace and the caption identified it as a piece of lace from a wedding dress. I thought about the dress I'd found and wondered if it was from the same one.

"Maybe someone decided to go on their miracle search in the attic," I said, bewildered. "Seems like all they'd find up there is a bunch of old stuff." I emphasized the word "stuff," not wanting Andy to think that I meant "junk." Andy was about to turn the page, but I stopped her.

"Okay, help me here. I don't get the lace thing. How is part of a wedding dress a miracle?"

"No clue," Andy said, as if it didn't interest her. "Katy probably went to the attic to let off steam."

I considered this. "Katy was probably the only one going off on the searches at her house."

"Mmm, doubt it. Remember Katy's letter that said they sent Uncle Glenn on a search? And my mom has made my Dad go off a couple of times, and Mom's gone off a few times too— once when Ben and Haley told her to."

"What?" I laughed. "The twins sent your mom on a miracle search?"

Andy nodded. "She was cranky one day after we moved in. I think it was seeing all of Aunt Dorothy's stuff, and Katy's old room. She was sad. Anyway, Ben and Haley told her she'd been yelling at them too much and needed to go on a search."

"And she did?"

"Uh huh. Dad kind of backed the twins. He encouraged Mom to go take walk, at least."

"I can't ever imagine telling your mom to go find a miracle. It seems so—" I couldn't find the word.

"It was the right thing to do though. Ben and Haley were right. She'd been impossible."

"It's hard to imagine your mom being anything but wonderful," I said. Andy only smiled and turned another page.

"What did she bring back?" I asked. Maybe I could get a clue; certainly Mrs. Skully knew what a real miracle was.

"I think it was a feather."

"A feather? Like a bird feather?"

"Yeah, I think so. She said she found it alongside the path toward the pond. Maybe a duck's."

Again, it didn't seem to bother Andy or make her wonder why a feather. I felt disappointed. There was no clue there.

And the Mason miracle book didn't reveal any clues for me that day either. Uncle Glenn's miracle was there—it looked to be some kind of leaf, or part of one. It was so old and crunchy-looking it was hard to tell. It was stapled in a piece of plastic, like the lace. I guess I'd been hoping that his miracle would at least tell me something. But with each page we found more things that made my uncertainty that much bigger. One page especially puzzled me. Stapled to the page was what looked like a deflated balloon, a card, and a piece of string.

The card read:

Marion Turner
561 Albert Street
Minneapolis, Minnesota
Age 12

My name is Marion. I sent this message off with the balloon

on September 20, 1959. If you find it, please write to me.

The caption read: "Found by Katy, October 14, 1959, in field near pond."

"Wow," I said to Andy, looking up from the book and re-alizing that it was getting dark inside the barn. "That card came all the way from Minnesota? In the air? By balloon?"

"Must've. I remember doing that in the sixth grade—send-ing balloon messages."

"Really? Did anyone ever get a letter back?"

"Just a few kids. But it was pretty exciting waiting to hear."

I was torn. The idea was neat—hoping for a pen pal from another town, another state. But a miracle? I tried to figure that maybe this was like the kite—and it involved wind, and that somehow God was guiding the balloon to someone who needed a pen pal. But when I thought I'd made the connection, it seemed as if I were really stretching it—like I was maybe making a connection instead of it really being there. I just couldn't tell.

I wanted to ask Andy, but she seemed so unaffected by it all—and she really didn't know. Nothing she said helped me, though she tried to answer all my questions. She seemed comfortable with the whole miracle thing.

There were other miracles, too, that surprised me and made no real sense. When Andy reached the last page and closed the book with a sort of satisfied finality, I found myself feeling more lost and not satisfied.

"Mom will love that we found this. Maybe we should head on back to the house and show it to her. It's getting dark in here."

We pushed the crates back, covered the sideboard, and I fol-lowed Andy out of the stall. We walked the length of the barn by the last light from the windows and the open doors at the end. We closed the doors and pulled down the long, heavy piece of wood to bolt them as we left.

Taking the path to the farmhouse, I could hear the crickets chirping and the bullfrogs from the pond, their croaking loud across the field on such a still evening. I breathed in the warmth of the evening, making me feel good. It struck me that for all the miracles and all the searches, and these two books, for me, maybe the one miracle I'd ever have in my life was being a part of the Skully family. Watching Andy ahead of me, I knew that it was true.

Chapter 11

That summer seemed fairly uneventful, but in looking back, I guess I was in the middle of some major life changes—or maybe transitions. Everything seemed uncertain and unsettled for me then. It mostly had to do with my mom, and trying to do what Andy's mom had said to me.

I watched my mom a lot after my birthday talk with Mrs. Skully. I guess I was trying to decide if she was, in fact, doing her best. I'm not sure I was ever able to tell. She still traveled a lot, and was still distracted by her job. And she didn't talk to me that much. But it was more than my dad did.

She tried to see that I had all the right clothes, even though she really didn't know what they were. And she asked me about Andy sometimes to make sure we were still friends. I'd watch her as she put on makeup and she'd ask, "Are you studying at Andy's tonight?" Or when she packed her suitcase for a business trip, "Are you spending the weekend with the Skullys?"

On one hand, I felt angry that she just assumed I'd be taken care of, knowing where I'd be staying. But then I tried to see it from Mrs. Skully's perspective—at least she did ask. I don't know. I don't think I ever resolved my feelings about Mom that summer. I just know that I felt a lot of turmoil about how I wanted to feel and how Mrs. Skully said I should try to feel.

Another thing that happened was Mrs. Skully made me go search for a miracle and I sort of rebelled about it. But she won, of course. I could never disrespect Mrs. Skully, though I think that day I came pretty close.

First, let me say I can get in quite a mood. It doesn't happen often, because usually I'm quiet when I'm upset, but once in a while I can be a real pain. Even Mrs. Gorkin knows that, but I try not to be like that around her. I was in such a mood the day Mrs. Skully made me search for a miracle. It stands out in my mind as the day I came a step closer—a real step—in understanding the whole idea of miracles and Mrs. Skully's searches.

"Darla," Mrs. Skully said to me one August afternoon, "why the long face? The boys are out ready to deliver a baby calf in the gray barn. It's a little unusual for it to be born this late in the summer. Don't you want to see it?" I was flopped out on the porch swing, one leg thrown over the arm. Andy was in the house getting something Jason needed in the barn. I was in a mood—and not one for talking.

"It's just so hot, Mrs. Skully. Too hot to move."

She considered this. "Are you sure that's it? It wasn't this hot yesterday, but I recall seeing you on that porch swing."

I felt irritated. I didn't want to talk about it. I didn't want to talk about anything. And what difference did it make to her if I was immobile or not? So I shrugged.

Mrs. Skully disappeared into the house and returned with two tall glasses of lemonade and her scrapbook stuff. I mumbled a quick "thanks" and took a glass.

She worked on her pictures for a while and left me alone. I was grateful for the silence. But it didn't last long.

"Did you ever see this picture of my mother, Darla?" She handed me a yellowed photo of a woman standing next to a tractor.

"No," I answered, not really looking at the picture.

"Someday you'll have to meet her. She's very interesting."

"Real nice, I bet. Like everyone in your family." I said this with just a slight tone of sarcasm. After I said it, I was instantly sorry. I knew Mrs. Skully had heard it.

"No, my mother's not always nice. But she certainly is

interesting." I didn't get it. "Interesting" seemed like an odd word to use for your mother, so she had my attention. "When I was growing up, we didn't really get along very well. She had seven other children to look out for and a large farm to run with my father."

"Were you ever close? I mean, like you and Andy?"

She shook her head. "Not really."

I looked at the scrapbook and wondered at the hours she'd spent putting it together. She tried to pick just the right pictures. All for a mother to whom she was not close. Like I said, I was in a mood. So I asked the most insensitive question I could.

"So why are you working so hard on something for someone you don't like very well?"

Mrs. Skully smiled. It was a patient smile. "I didn't say I didn't like her."

"You said you didn't get along with her very well." I was being obstinate.

"There's actually quite a difference." She looked at me for what seemed an eternity, a half-smile on her face. "Just because you don't get along with someone, Darla, doesn't necessarily mean you don't like them. Or love them, for that matter."

"Do you love your mom?"

"Yes, but that doesn't mean everything between us is always okay. I've just come to accept her as she is."

I took a drink of my lemonade and fell silent. I knew she was trying to tell me something. I mean, I'm pretty smart about stuff like that. I guess she was trying to make some kind of connection between me and my mom, and her and her own. I decided to show my intelligence.

"Well, I don't know if I'll ever be able to accept my mom. Which, in that case, if your theory is true, I may never know how to love her either."

I sounded so matter-of-fact. Smug. But that's when I saw the patience on Mrs. Skully's face dissolve and the look in her eyes harden a little.

"Darla," she said thoughtfully. I'll never forget how she said my name that day. So quietly, but in total command. "I think you need to find a miracle this afternoon. If you go now, you'll be back in plenty of time for supper. We're having hamburgers and potato salad."

There was no uncertainty in her voice. No hesitation. No crack in the door. For as cocky as I felt, Mrs. Skully had control. I knew I must go. But I wanted her to know that I perfectly understood what she was trying to do. That even though she was the adult, I wasn't stupid.

"Okay, Mrs. Skully," I said finally, setting my glass down on the porch floor and sitting up in the swing. "This is supposed to make me cool off, right? Give me time to sort things out? Blow of some *steam*?" I emphasized the word like I had it all figured out.

She stopped sorting through her pictures for a moment and looked off across the yard. "Hmm . . . . Well, I don't know. I hadn't thought of it that way. I guess that's one way of looking at it." It was a skeptical response, and obviously not what she'd had in mind. It bothered me that she hadn't taken the bait. I tried a question instead.

"Well, if you're not looking for me to come back in a better mood, then what? What's the miracle supposed to prove?"

This time she didn't look up. "You know, Darla, I can't really tell you. My children have to figure out about the miracles on their own."

I think it was the way she said "my children" that finally shut me up. It was hot and I felt like crying. Suddenly I wanted very much to hug her. I wanted to apologize. The fact that she might actually think of me as part of the family—as one of her own kids—sort of blew me away. And suddenly I didn't feel so intelligent. Or smug. I just felt ashamed and tired and sad. Like I said, I was in a real mood that day.

Mrs. Skully left, but soon returned with the Polaroid. She handed it to me. I wanted to ask her if it was okay if I took a picture of the calf being born, but I figured she'd say that it was a cop-out. And really it was . . . . except that it was a miracle— or seemed like one. The birth of anything was a miracle. A lot more than some old kite or pussy willow tree.

Chapter 12

I thought a lot about the miracles that afternoon as I went searching for mine. I kept trying to figure out what Mrs. Skully was sending me out looking for—or, well, any of her kids. See, they seemed to take it for granted—these miracle searches. And Andy, well, from her prespective, had it mostly figured out. But me, I'm the kind of person who always wants to know why I'm doing something—I want to understand the intent behind it all.

So as I walked down the path, through the field, and past a giant grove of apple trees on the Skully property, I tried to see it from Mrs. Skully's perspective. If I had a kid who was being grumpy—well, let's face it, pretty nasty—why would I send her out alone, armed with a camera, in search of a "miracle," which from the looks of it could be just about any weird thing the Skully kids wanted to take a picture of.

It just didn't seem to add up, especially if Andy's interpretation wasn't right. Hers sounded pretty reasonable, about blowing off steam. But Mrs. Skully seemed sort of puzzled by the idea. Like it had never occurred to her. See, she never made the Skully children explain what they picked. They never had to offer any explanation for what they found. Mrs. Skully just accepted each picture with a smile. So except for Andy's interpretation, I never got a sense of what her brothers were thinking about all of it—what they were getting out of it.

As I circled back and returned to the path, I stooped down and looked at the small stones and gravel that filled in with the bits of grass and weeds. I always liked rock collecting as a kid, and I still liked looking at them.

As I sifted through them, letting a handful fall in a scattered design on the path, one in particular caught my eye. It was light gray, with some quartz, and on one side what appeared to be some type of fossil. I tried to guess what kind of animal had lived and died on that rock—whose body had imprinted itself into the stone. I used to try and imagine those kinds of things a lot when I was a kid. I was very curious about what came before us in life. I decided that the animal in or on it might have been a centipede or something. It was sort of oblong and scaly-looking. I figured this would be the closest thing I was going to get to a miracle that afternoon—I mean, God created all animals, and this was proof that one had lived here. It was good enough, I thought. I figured Mrs. Skully would see the connection.

When I got back to the house, I showed Mrs. Skully the rock and she smiled in her usual gentle way and said that it would be a nice addition to the miracle book. She went to the kitchen and got a small plastic baggie and a stapler. She put the rock into the baggie and stapled the baggie to a page, making sure each side was securely fastened. Mrs. Skully tried to put the "real thing" in whenever a picture would not show it well enough.

In my desire to have her understand why I picked a rock, I must have mumbled something about animals, God, and miracles, because she looked at me with a quizzical smile.

"Why do you think a miracle is connected to God, Darla?"

I wasn't sure how to answer. It seemed so obvious. "Well," I started, "aren't miracles something that God makes happen?"

"Are they?" She had put the miracle book away and had started back on her scrapbook.

"Well, sure," I hesitated. "I mean, when babies are born, and people survive car crashes, or a tornado blows through a whole city without killing anyone, people say, 'It's a miracle.' And somebody or something was watching out for them." I hesitated again. "God."

Mrs. Skully nodded a puzzled nod and kept working. She'd left the door open for me and I was genuinely curious. "Well, if not God, what then?"

"Have you ever looked up the meaning of 'miracle' in the dictionary?"

I shook my head and mumbled that I hadn't.

"The dictionary's over there on the bookshelf. Why don't you see what it says?"

I took the book off the shelf and looked it up. I read aloud what it said: "An extraordinary event manifesting divine intervention in human affairs."

I looked at Mrs. Skully triumphantly, but she just smiled. "Keep reading."

"An extremely outstanding or unusual event, thing, or accomplishment."

I repeated the second definition slowly, and I think Mrs. Skully saw the puzzled look on my face.

"What is it, Darla?"

"Well," I said thoughtfully, trying to say what my head was thinking. "Then practically anything in the world could be considered a miracle, depending on how you look at it."

I knew I'd stumbled onto something, because for a brief moment I saw Mrs. Skully's smile widen. And it was sort of a knowing smile, a little to herself. And then it was gone. "I suppose you could be right about that, Darla—depending on how you look at it."

But I still didn't get it. Not really. I mean, if that's how Mrs. Skully looked at things—the world—well, I still couldn't figure why she sent her kids out looking for miracles, especially if they were so easy to come by, and God wasn't really involved after all.

Chapter 13

The last week of summer vacation, I started my period. I felt abandoned because my mom was in Houston and I really wanted to talk to her. It seemed like something I should be discussing with my own mother first. So, of course, I told Andy instead. When I told her, she threw her arms around me and laughed. "Join the ranks. Darla. You made it." And she grabbed my hand and pulled me downstairs to tell her mom.

I believe what scared me the most about telling Mrs. Skully was that I would finally see the separation between Mrs. Skully's real kids and me. That she wouldn't treat me the same as she had Andy when she got her period; after all, it was a pretty personal, mother-daughter thing. Family barbeques and sleepovers didn't automatically make me "family."

But Mrs. Skully hugged me close, gave me her usual warm smile, and then pulled out a lemon meringue pie from the frig. "I was saving this for dessert tonight," she grinned, "but I think this deserves celebrating."

We all sat down at the table and Mrs. Skully cut each of us a huge piece of the tangy pie. And as we sat talking, she asked me how I felt and if I needed anything, and that she'd been a "late bloomer" too. I think it was just about the best afternoon of my life—sitting there with Andy and her mom, eating pie, and feeling wrapped up in their love and care. For a moment, I felt like Mrs. Skully's daughter—a part of a family, a part of something wonderful. I never wanted it to end. But, the fire changed everything, and then, nothing was ever the same.

Chapter 14

When school started the following week, Andy and I both found ourselves adjusting to ninth grade and the new pressures of high school. We had three of our seven classes together, and lunch period, so we had a lot of time to pass notes and keep up on things.

After a few weeks, it seemed we were really beginning to adjust until I saw a poster on the wall that stopped my heart:

MOTHER-DAUGHTER DINNER BANQUET
SATURDAY, OCTOBER 5

I felt sick to my stomach, knowing that my mother was scheduled to be in Paris during October and wouldn't have been caught dead at a mother-daughter banquet anyway. Well, in all fairness, I wasn't positive my mom wouldn't be interested, but I was pretty sure. She'd never invited me out to lunch—you know, one of those "just girls" kind of things. A mother-daughter banquet was over the edge for my mom.

I felt really depressed and Andy noticed it during lunch. I'd hardly said a word to her all morning and I picked at my food after we'd sat down with our trays.

"What is it?" Andy urged, biting into her sandwich. She chewed methodically, never taking her eyes off my face, just patiently waiting for me to reply.

"It's nothing," I said matter-of-factly, trying to sound more cheery. I usually can fool people into believing everything's fine if I try hard enough. But Andy was always good at reading me, although sometimes she would leave me alone. Today, she wasn't so sure.

"What gives? You were fine yesterday. Didn't you pass Mr. Jacobson's pop quiz?"

I shrugged. "I got a B."

"Well, what then?"

"Look," I said pretty directly. "Let's change the subject." I could always be direct with Andy, and she let it go.

"Okay." She paused for a moment. "Did you see the posters for the mother-daughter banquet? Are you going?"

I wanted to say something sarcastic or laugh and remind Andy that my mom wasn't like hers, that I was surprised she didn't remember. I wanted to say, "Are you nuts?" Instead, I did something I'd never felt I had to do with Andy before. I lied.

"I'm not sure yet," I said, taking a long slurp of my milk. "I'm sure my mom would love to come to something like that. I'll just have to check with her about her schedule."

Andy nodded, accepting my lie without much question or comment. "I'm gonna ask my mom tonight. I hope she can go. I think she said something about visiting her sister Sheri sometime in October for her birthday."

I looked at Andy with open incredulity. "Of course your mom will go. She loves this kind of stuff. I'm sure it can't be the same weekend. Or she'll cancel."

Andy shrugged. "I'll have to check."

She didn't seem overly concerned, and I felt suddenly angry at her. Of course she didn't have to be concerned. Andy and her mom had all kinds of mother-daughter outings—what was one more? If they couldn't make it, well, what did it matter? At that moment, I felt like I was nobody's daughter, and I just wanted to be left alone. "Look," I said, my Saran Wrap and waxed paper making a soft crunching sound as I balled them up to throw away. "I've gotta study. I'm going over to the library for the rest of lunch period."

It was obvious that I didn't want Andy to join me, and she let me go, giving me a look that said she knew something was up, and that we'd talk later. That was the best part about Andy. She knew I'd need to talk about it later. And, of course, she'd be there when I was ready.

The next day at lunch Andy brought the subject up again, but now she'd figured some things out. And my lie got bigger.

"Let me guess," she said through a mouthful of macaroni and cheese. "Your mom can't go to the banquet." She looked concerned, but I couldn't stand that my family situation was so predictable, or that I was always some kind of orphan.

"Actually," I said somewhat smugly. "She can. I asked her last night."

"That's great!" Andy was enthusiastic, her eyes lighting up with real joy. "I'm happy for you." I felt ashamed. She didn't deserve the lie, and I had no way of knowing how I'd ever explain my way out of it the night of the banquet, when neither my mom nor I would be there.

"What are you wearing?" Andy asked, innocent to just how far the lie was going.

"I haven't decided yet. Are you dressing up?"

"Yeah, I guess. I'll probably wear a dress if that's what you mean."

I nodded and let the subject drop, but it was obvious that she was relieved that my mom was finally going to "be there" for me. But as lies usually do, mine came back to rat me out.

As the mother-daughter banquet got closer, Andy's mom was acting mysterious. I couldn't really explain it, but she seemed to purposely avoid the topic of the banquet. I felt like I knew Mrs. Skully as well as she knew me, and she seemed to be holding something back, but I couldn't figure what. I didn't realize at the time that her mystery would reveal my lies, and that the night of the mother-daughter banquet would turn out very different from what I expected.

The day before the banquet, Andy started acting funny. I

mean, like nothing ever before; there was something definitely up.

She wasn't exactly aloof, or mad. But she seemed sort of confused—maybe surprised. Quiet. When I asked her about it, she pulled one of my usual answers and said it was nothing. Suddenly she was going to the library during lunch period. It made me a little nervous, but I figured everyone was entitled to a few bad days. Besides, I was starting to feel lousy myself— partly because of the lies I'd told, and partly because I wasn't going to the banquet, something I really had wanted to do.

The day before the banquet, I was eating lunch outside when Andy sat down beside me and opened her lunch sack. It was obvious she was angry, because Andy's lips got really white when she was mad about something.

"What's the matter?" I asked, my voice a little shaky. I think I knew what was coming.

"Why didn't you tell me?" She might just as well have asked, "Why did you lie to me?"

I played dumb. "Tell you what?"

"Come on, Darla. What were you going to tell me tomorrow? That you suddenly got sick and couldn't go? That you had car trouble? Did you think I wouldn't find out?"

I was silent. I could feel my face turn red. I just wasn't sure how she'd found out. I looked down at my sandwich and said nothing. I felt sick. I'd never seen Andy this mad, never at me, and I began to wonder if she was going to stop being my friend. After all, a lie is a lie. I couldn't really blame her.

"Well," she said a little too loudly, "at least have the guts to be honest now." She was staring at me. She hadn't touched her food. I finally met her eyes and tried to explain.

"I don't know what I was going to tell you," I started, and then stopped. How could I tell her the mix of feelings that had caused the lies? Even I had trouble sorting them out. "I'm sorry I lied," I tried again.

"I don't really want your apology." She spat the words at

me. I was so shocked that for a moment I couldn't speak. I'd never seen her like this before.

"What do you want?" My sandwich seemed really dry and I choked a little on it.

"I want to know why you didn't just tell me that your mom was in Paris again. For Pete's sake, she's *always* in Paris. It's nothing new. You've told me all the other times she's been gone."

"True." Listening to her, seeing her so angry, I slowly felt steadier. Calmer. Suddenly I wanted very much to tell her. I wanted to make her understand, because I felt a little angry too. "And tell you the same stupid, boring story I tell you every time? So you can feel sorry for me? So the Skullys can come to the rescue and invite me to another of their family gatherings to make it up to me?"

I barely took a breath. "Maybe I just wanted to deal with this on my own. Because maybe I didn't want to admit how much I wanted to go to this stupid banquet. I'll be honest. I don't have a mother, Andy. I've tried to see her different—like your mom once told me I should—that my mom might just be doing the best she can. But it's not true. She's not doing anything at all."

The words poured out of me and I felt as if I couldn't stop. "I want something from my mom I can't have. And it's hard sometimes. It's just plain hard. And maybe I'm just sick of it."

She continued to look at me, but her lips weren't as white anymore. I can make quite a speech if the moment is right.

I let the silence linger momentarily, then I lowered my voice. "How did you find out?"

She answered right away—very matter-of-factly. "My mom called one afternoon to talk to yours—she wanted to buy corsages for us to wear to the banquet. Mrs. Gorkin answered. She said your mom was in Paris until the end of the month."

"I guess your mom was pretty mad at me when she found out I'd lied and everything."

"Not as mad as I was. She seemed to understand."

"Do you?" I looked at Andy carefully, studying her face. "I mean, do you understand?"

"Yeah," she answered, finally taking a bite of her sandwich. "It's hard to be mad at you. But I still am."

I nodded, letting the comment hang there between us. It seemed to move in, then out. Then away. We ate in silence for a long time.

When the five-minute warning bell rang, we packed up our stuff and headed toward the school. When we reached the doors, Andy asked, "So what are you doing tomorrow night?"

I shrugged. It seemed sort of irrelevant. "Maybe watch a video. I don't know."

"Well, I'll see you later."

"Hey, Andy," I said, and grabbed her arm. When she turned to look at me I didn't know what I wanted to say. "Sorry," came out, sort of lamely. She nodded and headed toward her class.

Chapter 15

All day Saturday I tried not to think about the banquet. Mrs. Gorkin dropped off the groceries and waxed the kitchen floor. When she finished, she knocked on my bedroom door and said goodbye for the rest of the weekend.

As soon as she left, I came out of my room, went downstairs, and flicked on the TV. There was a double creature-feature movie on, and I settled in with a giant bowl of popcorn. I spent the rest of the afternoon that way. The movies were actually pretty good, and I was able to block out the disappointment I was feeling about the banquet, the lies I'd told, and the whole lousy weekend.

At around six o'clock, I was trying to decide what to have for dinner, although I was pretty full from the popcorn, when the doorbell rang. I couldn't think of who it would be and I felt a little nervous being home alone. I went to the door and peeked through the hole. In the curved view of the peephole, I saw Andy and her mom standing there, all dressed up.

When I opened the door, I'm sure my face was a mix of surprise and awe. I looked at Andy and couldn't help but grin. "You guys clean up pretty good," I said, relieved and amazed to see them. I hadn't heard from Andy all day—which was unusual for a Saturday. And I was really glad to see her.

"Well, aren't you going to invite us in?" Mrs. Skully asked with a smile. She was carrying a box in her hands.

They both smelled of soap and perfume, and Andy's hair had been carefully curled. She was wearing a dress I'd never seen

before—black with little purple violets on it, pulled together at
the waist with a belt. It looked great on her. Mrs. Skully wore
a light pink blouse tucked into a navy blue skirt, with a pink
and blue flowered scarf at her neck. She had her hair pinned up
and looked really sophisticated.

"Wow, you guys really look great." I was a little embarrassed, unsure why they had come. They seemed to be waiting
for something. I turned down the TV and looked at them ex-
pectantly. Finally, Mrs. Skully spoke up.

"Darla, we want to invite you to the mother-daughter banquet. If you start now, you'll have time to get ready."

She said it so easily that I wasn't sure I'd heard her right.
I thought maybe they had stopped by to say hello for a minute
and cheer me up.

I looked at Andy, who smiled broadly. I could tell she wasn't
mad anymore. "Come on. I'll help you pick out something nice
to wear."

But I shook my head, finally processing what they were
saying to me. "Look, you guys are great. But this is a *mother-
daughter* banquet. I appreciate our stopping by, but—"

"Mom and I really want you to come with us," Andy said.

I had a sudden urge to point out the obvious—that I wasn't
a Skully. That I wasn't a daughter. That this was a family night.
That I was the odd-man-out. And I started to, but Mrs. Skully
cut me off—something she rarely did.

"Darla, we didn't come here because we feel sorry for you.
You've been a part of our family since we moved here. You
were a friend to Andy right from the start. I don't consider this
an act of charity, if that's what you're thinking. We're asking
you to come because we want you to share tonight with us."

But I said the obvious anyway. "Mrs. Skully, I'm not your
daughter. Not really. And besides, I'm sure the banquet com-
mittee didn't set an extra plate for a second Skully daughter."
I was feeling very self-conscious at that point. I knew they were
trying really hard, but I felt uncomfortable. But then Andy said

something that changed my mind. "You're the closest thing I've ever had to a sister. Most of the time I think of you as one, anyway. Which sort of makes you a daughter, well, by default."

Andy was always saying stuff like that—just like the first time we'd met, talking about midwestern towns. She had a way of making you stop and listen.

I didn't say anything, and Andy knew me well enough to know I was weakening. "So, get going," Andy finished. "We've got to be there by eight."

I hesitated, looking from Andy to Mrs. Skully, then back to Andy. Finally, I turned and went up the stairs to my bedroom. Andy followed, while Mrs. Skully sat down on the couch to wait.

I emerged about an hour or so later in a dress I usually wore to some rare social outing with my folks—it was a black dress with multicolored flowers on it, low-waisted, and a pair of black heels. I "borrowed" a gold chain from my mother's jewelry box, figuring it was the least she could do to contribute to the even-ing. Andy had put a cloth headband in my hair— the color of the peach flowers in my dress.

When I came down the stairs and into the living room, Mrs. Skully stood up and hugged me. "You look beautiful, Darla. Both of you girls look beautiful. Here," she said, taking the Polaroid from her purse. "Let me take some pictures before we go." And she smiled that smile that always made me feel spe-cial—wrapped up in Skully love—and uncomfortable too. I wasn't used to a lot of affection.

It wasn't until about a month later—I guess it was nearing Thanksgiving—that I saw the pictures. Actually, I'd forgotten that Mrs. Skully had taken them. But it was during a miracle search, when Mrs. Skully was putting one of Ben's miracles into the book, that I looked over her shoulder and saw a picture of Andy and me in our mother-daughter banquet dresses, on the opposite page.

It struck me so odd, caught me off guard, that I momentarily lost track of the conversation. Two different emotions took hold of me: the first was an overwhelming feeling of surprise. That I would mean enough to them to hold a spot in such a meaningful book, but the second feeling followed so closely that it was hard to differentiate the two. Why would a picture of Andy and me be in the miracle book? From whose search did it come?

As hard as I tried, I just couldn't figure it. I mean, I guess we could be considered miracles because we're human beings, born into the world, and God, of course, was supposed to have something to do with birth and all that stuff. But beyond that, it didn't make a whole lot of sense to me.

Yet something in me decided not to ask Mrs. Skully about it. I think I wanted to enjoy the fact that someone considered me a miracle, for I couldn't recall a feeling finer or mixed with such sweet surprise as seeing my face next to Andy's that day in the miracle book.

Chapter 16

As the Christmas holidays approached, I felt a joy for the season I had never quite known before. The Skullys were decorating their tree about three weeks before Christmas, and they invited me to share in it with them. It was unlike anything I'd ever experienced.

Mr. Skully built a fire in the fireplace and, earlier in the day, he'd brought the decorations from the basement. The dining room table was piled high with boxes of tinsel, balls, bells, lights, and lots of colorful ornaments.

Mrs. Skully made hot cider and brought in steaming mugs with cinnamon sticks for all of us. I can still remember that smell now, whenever I smell a Christmas tree. She also popped large bowls of popcorn and brought them into the living room with a tray of needles and long pieces of string threaded through them.

The whole family joined in untangling the strings of lights, although Mrs. Skully had carefully wound them around pieces of cardboard the year before. Bad bulbs were replaced as each string was tested, and there was a lot of good-natured teasing and joking as Mrs. Skully and Andy tried to hide the white bulb that made the lights blink, and the boys and Mr. Skully kept putting it back in. I don't remember who won, but Andy winked at me and said they went through this every year.

Later, Andy gave me my Christmas present. It was the picture of the mother and daughter dancing in the rain—the one I'd found in the attic. She apologized for not buying me anything at a store, but she figured a "homemade" present was better. I hugged her and told her it was the best present I could think of.

It never occurred to me that evening, as we sang Christmas carols and trimmed the tree, that like the decorations and ornaments, some that were very old—passed down through the Skully family—so too were the lights that we strung around the tree. The police report attributed the fire to those lights—"faulty wiring" they said, caused a short to send the tree up in flames. Even now, I can remember that night and the cold reality of the morning after. It's something a person never forgets.

"Darla! Wake up!" My mother's voice whispered impatiently to me in the semi-darkness. I glanced at the digital clock on my nightstand: 2:08 a.m.

"What's the matter?" I asked her. I was pretty groggy but could sense the urgency in her voice. She looked a little ghostly standing over my bed in the light coming from the hallway. She had her white winter coat on—something I thought strange at two in the morning.

Words started to tumble from my mother's mouth, something that seemed to happen automatically when she was nervous or scared. "Get up and get dressed." She flicked on the overhead light and I blinked, squinting to bring her more fully into focus. "I was coming back from the Emersons—you know, their party was tonight. I was halfway down Green Road, but I couldn't go any farther. It was blocked off by fire trucks and policemen—they had set up orange cones and blockades across the entire street. The sky was all lit up, and people were coming out of their houses in their nightgowns and—"

"Mother," I said, getting out of bed and taking her by the shoulders. "What happened?"

She looked at me with a look of compassion and fear. She gently touched my arm—a touch I can still feel, as she rarely displayed affection that way—then she said, "There's a house on fire, down the street. I'm almost positive it's the Skully's."

I don't remember how I got dressed or found my shoes or managed to dig my ear muffs out of the box in the closet, but I remember my mother saying she'd drive me, and a feeling of deep gratitude flowing through me at that moment.

As we approached Green Road, I could see that it was indeed the Skully house that was on fire. Swinging open the car door before my mother had stopped, I jumped out, running toward the house that had been the only real home I'd ever known. All I could think was that they were all dead, and dark, scary visions crept into my head as I went running down the side of the road. I screamed for Andy as I came closer to the fire.

As I neared the house, I slowed down to a walk—it felt as if I crawled the rest of the way in slow motion as I felt the heat from the fire. Flames shot through the windows and licked the night air with a fury I'd seen only in movies. The firemen's hoses blasted streams of water into the windows, but they didn't seem to make any difference. Smoke danced and twirled into the night sky, the gray against black sending chills through me.

I stood horrified, paralyzed for an eternity. The air was thick with the smell of burning wood—and I almost thought I could smell all the good things in the Skully house burning as well.

I heard crying, which pulled my attention away from the fire to look for the Skullys. A cold shiver went through me when I didn't see them at first. Instead, I saw the flashing lights of an ambulance and I broke out in a cold sweat. But a moment later, I saw Andy, huddled in a blanket across the street, watching her house die. She looked sick in the yellow-orange light.

"Andy!" I screamed, running across the street and dodging fire hoses to get to her. She turned to me and I caught her in my arms as she buried her face in my shoulder, sobbing. I held her as she said over and over, "Everything's gone. All gone. I can't believe this."

"Andy," I said finally, pulling her back by the shoulders and making her face me. "What about your family? Is everyone okay?" I could hardly get the words out.

For a moment she seemed too dazed to answer. She just looked at me and then back at the house, shaking her head.

"Andy!" I shook her. "Is everyone okay?" She nodded slightly and pointed. A few feet away, the rest of the family huddled together as people brought them coats and blankets. The looks of disbelief on the Skully faces were coupled with terror. They all just stared at their house and cried together.

I suppose it was some kind of miracle that they all got out alive. Yes, this was a miracle, I thought ironically. This I understood as something special, meaningful, even though the entire house was gone. At least they were all alive.

I looked back and forth at the faces of the Skully family. Their eyes were glazed over—the firelight reflected back in those vacant, wet stares. Their faces were lit by a frightening white, yellow-orange glow, making them look waxy and mannequin-like. I couldn't help feeling something else was wrong, and it was nagging me.

It wasn't until I heard the twins crying that I figured it out, because it was Jason who bent down to console them, not Mrs. Skully. I realized then that she was standing apart from her family, farther back in the darkness, her hand covering her mouth. She was staring blankly at what was once her home. There were no tears in her eyes. The look of devastation was complete.

I wanted to go to her, to hold her—and a part of me wanted to cling to her too. I wanted to say it would be all right, even though I didn't believe it. And I wanted to say how much I loved her. But I stayed where I was, hugging Andy. Suddenly I was scared for both of us.

Those hours before morning seemed to rush past in a blur. My feet were numb, but I really didn't notice until people started moving away and back to their homes. It wasn't until then that I remembered to invite the Skullys to stay at our house, a thought I'd had hours before. But it seemed that everyone else on the block had already done so. When I mentioned it to Andy, she motioned for me to ask her dad, but when I approached Mr.

Skully, he said they were staying with the Petersons across the street. It was clear that he meant the entire family, so I didn't ask him if Andy could stay with me. And it seemed logical; in a family crisis, you need your family to stick together.

I watched them all being led away to the Petersons. People were gentle, speaking softly. Someone had brought the smaller boys coats to put on—all too big, and Mrs. Skully had on a parka with a lot of fur around the hood. Still, she stood apart. She was the last to leave.

When I finally turned away and started to walk back toward home, I looked up to see my mother walking toward me with a blanket in her arms. I remember thinking that it was the lap blanket from the trunk, the red and black checkered flannel one she took to football games when she and Dad could make them at the university. It stood out darkly against her white winter coat. She'd gone home and changed out of her heels, wearing now a pair of old sweat pants and some boots. Seeing her there threw me almost as much as the fire. I didn't know what to do.

Suddenly I found myself running to her in the darkness, slipping on the icy road until I felt her arms around me. I buried myself against her, feeling a warmth in her hug that I'd never known, and being incredibly thankful and surprised that she was there to hold me.

Chapter 17

The next morning I rode my bike across the icy road to the Skully home. I'd slept maybe an hour or two, and felt sick and lost. I knew I had to go back. I propped my bike against a tree and stood there, looking at the dark, black window eyes of the house. It was gutted, the frame and outside walls left standing. Through the opening where the door had been, I could see light.

I glanced over my shoulder at the Peterson's house, but all the blinds were shut. If I knew Mrs. Peterson, she'd have given them all hot cocoa and sent them to bed. Hopefully, they'd had more sleep than I'd had.

I felt like a trespasser, but I really wanted to go through that open doorway into the Skully house. It seemed important. It was like I wanted to do it before they had to—to soften the blow somehow. Or maybe to still feel a part of the family that once lived there.

As I approached the house, it struck me that the front porch was still there. It wasn't really that burned. It was weird. It was almost as if I could take my bike up the steps and park it there, just as I always had.

As I walked through the threshold, I had an instant feeling of being torn apart. Though I'd watched the fire until it had smoldered to a close, nothing prepared me for what I saw.

Everything was black, charred and burnt, glistening under a coat of frozen water. The couch and chairs in the living room were gone, except for their metal frames. The cuckoo clock hung burned and cracked on the wall, ready to fall at any moment. The dining room table was broken in two, the legs burned into crispy cylinder cones. The hutch, where Mrs. Skully kept the china, was tipped over, and pieces of plates, cups, and saucers were strewn over the floor. I bent down and picked up a piece of a plate with the cornflower blue pattern that had been Mrs. Skully's great-grandmother's. I didn't see one piece that had survived intact. The memory of eating on those plates during one of the Skully parties nearly brought me to tears.

I walked through the kitchen door, but after looking at the mess there, I turned and went back into the living room. It was too much. Too enormous to be true. I stood in the middle of what had been the living room and looked at how the stairs to the bedrooms on the second floor led to sunlight. They were only partially there—and then they just fell away. I walked over to the doorway and looked up, following the stairs until I saw blue sky. It seemed like something from a horror movie. I thought of the song, "Stairway to Heaven," and I might have laughed at the thought if the sight hadn't made me choke back tears.

All the picture frames on the walls that were a history of the Skully family—Haley and Ben on their first two-wheelers, waving at the camera, Jason's with his second-place trophy in baseball the previous year, Andy in her choir gown; and the others—all gone. There were charred remnants of the frames scattered around the floor, but without pictures. It was at that moment, when I felt so deeply the loss of the family history, that I remembered the miracle book.

I picked my way back into the dining room to see if the little cabinet and shelves where Mrs. Skully kept the book and the Polaroid remained. But no; the cabinet had fallen on its side, and the doors were gone. Anything that had been inside was no longer there. I looked at the floor and saw what looked to be a part of the Polaroid, but no book.

Strewn around the floor were pieces and remnants of everything in the house: melted remains of the phone, the broken pot of Mrs. Skully's palm, pieces of glass from the mirror that had hung on the wall, a brass candlestick holder, a broken glass vase—

everywhere I looked, it was like a junkyard. I could hardly take it all in. Everything triggered a memory.

I stood there for a long time. The lighting seemed eerie. It was coming in from all the wrong places, going in all the wrong directions. I felt afraid; it was spooky in the Skully house. I took one last look and left, walking back through the rubble and out the front door opening.

As I came down the porch steps, I pulled the collar of my coat close around my neck against the cold. I blinked in the bright sunlight, its reflection against the snow making it hard to see. When I looked up, I was startled to see Mrs. Skully sitting against a tree across the street. She was wearing the same parka from the night before and had a blanket wrapped around her. I thought she must be freezing.

She didn't seem to see me at first. I waved to her, tentatively, but she didn't wave back. She looked small and fragile huddled under the blanket. I didn't see any of the other Skullys and there didn't seem to be any sign of life at the Peterson's. I glanced at my watch. It was only 9:30; I figured they were all still asleep.

I moved slowly down the stairs and down the front walk, slick and frozen from all the water from the fire hoses. I crossed the street, my hands shoved deep into my coat pockets. Still, Mrs. Skully didn't seem to see me. She just stared straight ahead, looking at what was left of the house. Looking past it.

"Mrs. Skully?" I didn't know what to say. She looked cold sitting there. "I . . . . I'm sorry. About everything."

"Hello, Darla." Her voice was flat. Lifeless. Her face offered no expression. She didn't even look at me when she spoke. I felt a chill go through me that had nothing to do with the cold.

"Mrs. Skully? Is there anything I can do?" She barely shook her head, hardly acknowledging the offer.

I could have handled her not smiling. But it was her eyes that terrifed me. They had always smiled. Even when she wasn't smiling with her mouth, her eyes smiled. They were happy. They were filled with love. Now, they were just empty.

I shifted from one foot to another, feeling uncomfortable. Mrs. Skully had always been able to put me at ease. She could do it with a look. A word. But she wasn't doing it now. She wasn't even trying. So I tried again.

"You must feel really bad, Mrs. Skully. I'm sure my father can give you some money—you know—to . . . . "

"Money can never replace what was in that house." The funny thing was, she didn't seem to be talking to me. Even though she'd responded to my voice, she wasn't talking to me. She seemed to be talking more to herelf. Or maybe she was talking to God.

"No, I guess not," I answered her, remembering the broken picture frames and china.

"Everything's gone. It's gone. It's all gone. There's nothing left." I think she might have cried then, but she seemed to be all cried out. Or maybe she hadn't even begun to cry.

"You can rebuild the house; we'll all be glad to help." My voice shook and I felt sick. I didn't know Mrs. Skully this way. Her face was pale and her eyes seemed to be set deep into her face. Dark circles were beginning to show beneath them.

But she was shaking her head, an ironic half-smile on her lips. "We can't rebuild our home."

I didn't know what to do. I felt panicky. I tried to remember the last conversation that I'd had with her. I needed to hear the friendly voice I'd become so accustomed to. I felt a piece of security falling away—something I had come to depend on in the last year. It surprised me how big of a hole it left in me now that I no longer felt it.

"Mrs. Skully, it will be okay." My voice shook again.

Then she answered in a voice I'll never forget. "It won't be okay. Nothing will ever be okay again."

I think my mouth fell open then. I'd never heard such sadness, regret or bitterness in anyone's voice—and especially never in Mrs. Skully's. Like there was no hope.

"It has to be," I went on, trying to sound brave. "I mean,

we'll all help you. You can all stay at our house." She was silent for a moment, and then she threw her head back and laughed. It was a hysterical laugh—but filled with grief. She laughed for a long time.

"Can you imagine all of us descending on your parents?" she said with a harsh laugh. "Oh, my goodness!" And she continued laughing, until she suddenly burst into tears, burying her head in her arms, her laughter turning to sobs.

I was numb. I felt an ache inside me so deep I thought I would die. She was like a completely different person. Lost. I felt near hysteria myself as I watched her—I felt paralyzed. I wanted desperately to help. But I also felt angry at what she had said. I knew I was supposed to ignore it, because she was in so much pain. But her comment about my parents got under my skin. I think a little of the anger won out just then. "At least everyone is safe. I mean, your kids and your husband— they're alive. It's a miracle no one was hurt."

"A miracle," she spat. "Some miracle. Look at it, Darla. Look at it!" She pointed at the house. She didn't even acknowledge what I'd said.

Then I felt an anger as I'd never known. How could she be so flip about the lives of her family? How could she place more importance on the house than the people who lived in it?

But as I watched her, my anger died away as quickly as it had come. I don't think I'd ever seen true despair on anyone's face, except a hungry child in a magazine. But it was there in the eyes of the woman I'd come to think of as my real mom. And it was real, and deep.

I felt like crying too, but it didn't seem right. She had fallen completely apart, had reached her point of no return. And I was scrambling to find a way to bring her back. I started thinking about the miracle book and all the things that mattered to Mrs. Skully. All the sentimental things that made her home so filled with love and meaning. And I thought about everything she'd lost the night before—all the remnants of those memories. It was pretty overwhelming. I felt a sorrow in my heart—for Andy, for Mrs. Skully, for all of them. But it was as if Mrs. Skully had given up. Completely. And that I could not handle.

I searched through the memories of my times at the Skullys for something, anything to pull her spirits from such darkness. Something to mention, to bring her back. It seemed it would take a miracle.

A miracle! I smiled a little to myself. I knew. I'd seen it in the ruins of the house. I had just the thing. Maybe. But I didn't know what to do. Ironically, it was Mrs. Skully herself who led me to the right path.

"All that ever meant anything to me was in that house," she said in a monotone. "My life was in there."

With that comment, I felt angry again. I thought I might explode. And then I did. "Everything you ever loved is sleeping in Mrs. Peterson's house!" I snapped, my voice full of emotion. "As for your life, well, you look pretty alive to me!" My face was flushed and I felt suddenly like an adult talking to a child. When Mrs. Skully looked up at me, squinting against the morning sunlight, I felt scared to be talking to her that way, but I kept on. I was mad at her.

"I . . . . I think, Mrs. Skully," I stammered, looking straight into her eyes, "that you need to go find a miracle." I said it matter-of-factly, the way she would have, and there was surprisingly no trace of uncertainty in my voice.

She stared at me, brows knitted in question, but with an expression asking me to explain. "I mean it, Mrs. Skully. I think . . . . you should go in search of a miracle. I'll . . . . I'll even help you."

"Darla, what are you talking about?" she said finally, finding her voice. She looked straight at me. Through me. I swallowed hard. My throat felt dry. "I think you need to go find a miracle. You know, the way you always have us do." And before she could respond, I put out my hands and took hers from her pockets, pulling her to her feet. "Come on, I'll help you."

She walked a few steps before coming to her senses. She stopped and stared at me, incredulous. "There are no miracles in there." But I pulled her along anyway, as if leading a child through a dark, frightening hallway.

She took the porch stairs but hesitated, then stopped at the entrance to the house. She shifted the blanket on her shoulders and fresh tears formed in the corners of her eyes. I could see it was killing her to go in.

I stepped through the doorway first, then silently coached her to follow me, kicking at the debris to make a path for her. As she entered the living room, she gasped, her eyes taking in the destruction. It looked like a wrecking ball had gone through. Paralyzed, she just stood there, her face like paste. She started to shiver beneath the parka and blanket, and I thought she might faint. I put my arm around her and waited for the horror to pass.

When she felt able to walk again, she moved away from me and wandered from room to room. She stayed a long time in the kitchen, and I didn't follow her. I could see her through the open doorway, moving around, looking at where things used to be. When she came out, she bent down to pick up a piece of the cornflower blue-patterned china, as I had. A little cry escaped her, and she looked at me then, almost accusingly, her eyes saying that there was nothing here—no miracle. That everything was gone.

"Mrs. Skully," I said. My words came out in a frozen rush. "Come here. I want to show you something."

She stood up and came toward me, her face a white mask of doubt. Beneath the blanket she seemed smaller, less capable than all the days and nights I'd seen her walk through that same dining room. She no longer felt its comfort. It was no longer hers.

I was standing in the living room, but all the rooms had sort of melted together. Mrs. Skully picked her way through the charred wood and wreckage to stand next to me. She spoke in a very tired voice. "Where's the miracle, Darla? I sure don't see one in here."

I bent down and pushed through the rubble, finally finding what I was looking for beneath a burned and charred piece of tabletop; maybe it was the tabletop that had kept it from being ruined by the fire.

A corner of the tin box that Mrs. Skully had kept the old family pictures in, the ones she was using for her mother's surprise scrapbook, was sticking out of the mess. It was charred and dented, but you could still recognize the flowered pattern of the tin.

I held it up triumphantly and watched her face. At first it didn't seem to register. She seemed foggy and unwilling to accept that anything of value could be salvaged from the disaster. But slowly, she seemed to acknowledge the box. I held out to her. She shook her head a little, and then looked at me with what I thought was hope. "Are there any left?" I said I didn't know, but moved close to her as I pulled off the lid. She stood perfectly still, watching me, waiting. It felt like enormous things were wrapped up in that moment, and that I had the key to all of them.

I opened the tin and held it out to her. Mrs. Skully took it from me and looked in. The pictures seemed to be okay. She took them out, and although they seemed a little wrinkled, as if they'd been close to the heat, they had somehow escaped the flames. She held them in her hands, looking at them for a long time, shuffling them. Then she broke down and cried, holding the pictures and tin in one hand, and burying her face in the other. As I moved to put my arm round her, she pulled me to her, sobbing against my chest. "Oh, Darla," was all she said.

It was while I was standing there in the wreckage, holding Mrs. Skully, that I realized I had been missing the point about the miracles all along—at least part of it. I'd spent so much time focused on trying to figure out why Mrs. Skully sent us on the searches that I'd failed to see a more important part of it—a part that I'd stumbled on during the summer but hadn't figured out; a part that really had been written right in the dictionary.

Sure Mrs. Skully may have sent us out on those miracle

searches to blow off steam, or to move past the thing that was bothering us, or to change our perspective, but that really wasn't it. She wanted us to go looking for a miracle because she'd long since figured out that anywhere you looked, everywhere you looked, in any situation, in any circumstance, you could find one. No matter what happened or how bad it all seemed, all you had to do was look and you could find something worth letting it go for. The world really was full of miracles—ordinary things that you might otherwise pass by if you didn't stop and really look. Things that made the problem you were facing seem very small and pretty insignificant because the world was so much bigger, and all you had to do was step outside the circle you were standing in to realize it.

Maybe at first Mrs. Skully couldn't believe that there was anything closely resembling a miracle in the burned farmhouse that had been her home since she'd been a child. But just finding the tin in the wreckage, in the horror of it all, was enough to remind her. But just as I thought I'd finally figured it all out, Mrs. Skully threw me a final curve—a curve that brought my life into focus in a way it never had been before.

She hung on me the same way that Andy had the day we'd talked about Darrell—like she was drowning and needed me to save her. Mrs. Skully felt heavy in my arms as she cried, but it was okay. I think she needed to cry, really cry. Because it was obvious that she had everything in the world bottled up inside of her and it needed to come out. I held her for a long time and hoped that when it was over—when she was finished crying—I might have a piece of the real Mrs. Skully back.

I don't know how long we stood there, but after awhile Mrs. Skully pulled back, searching her pocket for a tissue. When she didn't find one, I dug into my pocket and came up with an old one. I didn't know what to say. "It's probably used," I said.

She smiled at that and then sort of chuckled, nodding, using it anyway. It seemed to break the spell, helped divert her attention, and she blew her nose, wiping at her eyes. When she was finished, she looked up and sighed, taking in the room again. She just stood there, looking, and I didn't say anything. I let her come to terms with it in her own way.

I watched her look around the floor, at the ruins. She kicked at the rubble at her feet, shaking her head. Sometimes it seemed she couldn't take it in fast enough, at other times, she would stop and just stare at some indiscernible object for a long time. I put my arm across her shoulder and we just stood there.

When I thought she might never speak again, she turned and looked at me, her face softer now, her eyes a little clearer. She stared at me with what I couldn't quite call a smile, but her eyes were warmer. They were speaking. I stopped shivering a little, finally feeling a tiny piece of the Mrs. Skully I knew returning. But her face took me by surprise. It had the same look that Andy's had the day we'd talked about Darrel. It was gratitude. Or thankfulness. Or something warm and meaningful that I couldn't quite read. It seemed to be a look of friendship.

"You know, Darla," she said quietly, then stopped, still looking at me, reaching over to push a strand of hair out of my eyes. When she continued she spoke quietly, haltingly, her eyes looking at me very deeply. "I guess you don't always have to go searching for a miracle. Sometimes, one comes to you." She cupped my chin in her hand, and I looked at her in silence. In confusion. But she smiled. A real smile, although it was lopsided and said, "Sometimes one finds you when you least expect it."

She looked at me for the longest time, and for a moment I thought back to the day I'd seen my picture in the miracle book, unable to understand then how I fit in there, unable to accept that I belonged there.

Standing there that cold winter morning, in the charred remains of a house that had been my home, I stopped feeling so cold. A moment of warmth flowed through me as I acknowledged her appreciation of me. Just me. For who I was. I realized that I meant something important to her, and it was the greatest feeling I've ever had.

Very gently, I took the pictures from her and put them back into the tin, placing the lid on carefully. Then turning to put my arm around her shoulders, I gently walked Mrs. Skully out of that house on Green Road, into the bright light of the morning.

Epilogue

Three years have passed since the fire at the Skully house. Maybe it was the graduation card I got from Mrs. Skully this week wishing she and Andy could be in the bleachers Saturday when I receive my diploma that brought it all back to me. It should have been Andy and me getting our diplomas together.

Whenever I ride down Green Road, either on my bike or in the car, I sometimes stop and look at the new house that was built by a new family on the Skully property. It was Mrs. Skully who decided not to rebuild the farmhouse, saying that perhaps it was time to let the farm go. I think she meant that it had been a great place in its day, but that it has seen enough tragedy for its lifetime. So they sold the property.

Andy's dad moved the family in temporarily with his brother-in-law in West Branch and took a job there. West Branch was about three hours away from me, so I started to see Andy less and less. The Skullys came back to visit every so often, but I don't see Andy much anymore.

In the early spring after the fire, I went to the woods on the Skully property and picked a huge bouquet of pussy willows and brought them home to my room. My mother saw me come in with them and got a vase from the china cabinet. I kept them for a long time.

Pussy willows are quite amazing, really. If you take some time to truly look at them, they have these hard little shells— dark brown, about the size of a small fingernail—but from them bloom these incredibly soft and delicate balls of fluff. They're grayish-white, almost the color of pearl, and they're soft like rabbit fur. I understand why one can consider them miracles.

Life is funny—sometimes it provides really special, beautiful things beneath a hard, tough exterior. And you never know they're there unless you are willing to wait long enough for them to bloom.

You can't find pussy willows very easily. It's not like they grow in every field or can be found like dandelions in the yard. And I think that's what makes them so unique—they're special and they're not like anything else. If you come across them, it's almost impossible not to stop and take a look. I can't pick pussy willows or look at them now without remembering the pussy willows in the miracle book. And though I can no longer just go to the Skully property and pick them from the tree as I did the year after the fire, I try to keep a bouquet of pussy willows in my room as often as I can. I know that when I have my own home someday, it'll have pussy willow trees in the yard the way Andy's house had apple trees.

Picking them that spring after the fire, I was amazed to find that the pussy willows were blooming in the snow. It was early March and there had been a typical Michigan winter— a thaw in January, a deep freeze in February, and then more snow in March. I wasn't really sure that there would be any pussy willows in bloom, even though Mrs. Skully had told me once that they were at their best in March.

But when I went walking along the Skully property after school one March afternoon, searching for the tree that Mrs. Skully had told me was near the edge of the field, I found them. They were indeed in bloom—little caps of snow covered each bloom like a tiny white hat. And as I cut each branch, the snow fell away, leaving the soft pearl-like fur exposed.

It was hard to imagine that anything so delicate and so beautiful could bloom in the cold that way, but the pussy willows seemed oblivious to their environment, bursting forth their softness as if to say that regardless of what the day brought, or whether it was sunny or snowing, they would bloom anyway. No matter what.

Well, the day I got the card from Mrs. Skully, Mom took me school shopping and had been talking a lot about the university she attended. She's determined to help make my "college experience," as she puts it, as good as her own and seems almost as excited as I am. She even talks about taking me to Paris with her when I come home for winter break. She says it's so that I can see "what she does" in her job. But I actually think she wants me to be with her. I think it might be a fun trip, maybe, to create some of those family memories I was so hot about.

We never found the Skully's miracle book—those miracles are only memories now for me. The Mason's book was lost in the fire too. And for a long time, that really bothered me. But lately, I find myself searching for miracles on my own, looking for them in my daily life. Even though I haven't created a miracle book like the Skully's, I've made my own book in my head and it's just as good. Just yesterday, I took a mental picture of the swans and their signets at the pond behind our house.

As long as we've lived in that house, we've never had swans. But this year they came. And last month I found this huge pine cone when I was riding my bike through the trails down near the river park. I stopped to pick it up and later put it on the shelf in my bedroom. It was bigger than a softball and I almost ran over it—it was just there, in the middle of the trail. And of course, whenever I see a pussy willow tree, I take a mental picture of that, too, and I can't help but smile.